# Jackie of all Trades: Mistress of None

## CHRITA PAULIN

Copyright © 2018 Chrita Paulin

All rights reserved. No parts of this book may be reproduced, stored, or introduced into a retrieval system, or transmitted in any form or by any means (electronic, mechanical, photocopying, recording, or otherwise), without the prior written permission of both the copyright owner and the above publisher of this book, except in the case of brief excerpts in critical reviews and articles.

The incidents, characters, and events have been presented to the best of the author's memories. The memories and perceptions of others may differ. Some names and identifying details may have been changed to protect the privacy of individuals. Every effort has been made to make this book as complete and accurate as possible, but no warranty is implied. The authors and the publisher shall have neither liability, nor responsibility, to any person or entity with respect to any loss or damages arising from the information contained in this book.

Published in the United States by Coal Under Pressure, LLC

Editor: Spurgeon Thomas

Cover Art Photography and Design: Zariah Paulin

Library of Congress Control Number: 2018938519

ISBN-13: 978-1-7326303-2-1

www.coalunderpressure.com

To my husband, Terrance:

I wrote my portion of this book in two days, yet have spent a week trying to find the right words for my dedication. I struggle because there aren't enough words to express the depths of my love for you. You came in to my life and taught me to dream beyond borders. You helped me shed my fear and enjoy life in ways I did not know was humanly possible. I sit in awe each day as I watch you with our children: nurturing, teaching, inspiring. You are a great father, an even greater husband. You give me purpose. You fuel my passion to succeed.

I thank you for being my rock and my feather. I thank you for reminding me my dreams and goals are important. Simply put, I thank you for loving me like no one else can.

# Contents

| | | |
|---|---|---|
| | Foreword | i |
| | Preface | v |
| | Acknowledgements | vii |
| CHAPTER 1 | JACKIE OF ALL TRADES: MISTRESS OF NONE | 1 |
| CHAPTER 2 | BROKENNESS, BAGGAGE AND BLESSINGS | 13 |
| CHAPTER 3 | IN THE MIDST OF MY RESISTANCE: DESIGNED ON PURPOSE | 27 |
| CHAPTER 4 | THE DAY I MET MYSELF | 39 |
| CHAPTER 5 | F_CK POSITIVITY: MAKE SHIT HAPPEN! | 53 |

# Foreword

"Mama, I wanna be a writer."

I announced this to my mother when I was nine years old. That warm summer evening, she and my father sat on the porch chairs talking and enjoying the slight cool breeze, and I was where every young child had to be when the street lights came on back then—on our front steps. But unlike most kids, I wasn't playing a game or pouting about not being able to run around. I was reading a short story in one of my mother's *Reader's Digest* magazines. I can't recall the author, the title, or even what the story was about. I just remember that at the end of the story, I looked at the words. I didn't read them again. I kept turning the pages and looking at the words, and this feeling, this passion came over me that said, Hey! I wanna do that. The thought of putting words on paper that make someone see, hear, feel, taste, and smell things and people that aren't actually there, go places, while sitting on her front steps was the coolest thing that had ever come to my mind.

Now at nine years old, I didn't have the vocabulary to articulate all of what I was feeling, so I simply said, "Mama, I wanna be a writer."

My father smiled and my mother simply said, "Well, write, baby," as if there was nothing in the world that could come between me and my dream of becoming a writer.

With my father's proud smile and my mother's encouraging words, I was off. I started writing short stories, which boosted my confidence in my ability to tell a good story. The more I wrote and the more I read, the more passionate I became about writing. Fast forward several years, while being a wife to a wonderfully loving and supportive husband, and a mother to three beautiful children, I received my B.A. in English from Coppin State University and my M.A. in Literature from the University of Maryland at College Park. My first novel, *Water In A Broken Glass*, received the Just About Books Annual Book

Award, captured the #6 spot on the On-Demand Best Seller list, is ranked #17 on Accredited Online Colleges' 20 Essential Novels For African-American Women list, was recorded for the Maryland School for the Blind, is included in The Greenwood Encyclopedia of Multiethnic American Literature, Ethnic American Literature: An Encyclopedia for Students, and Black Like Us: A Century of Lesbian, Gay, and Bisexual African American Fiction. *Water In A Broken Glass* is now a feature film of the same title. My second novel, *In the Mirror*, received the African American Expo Award for Fiction. Currently, I am in the process of querying agents for my third novel, *Kizmic Journey*, and I'm writing my fourth novel, *The Subway*. I am a proud, longstanding member of the Black Writers Guild of Maryland. And lastly, along with my husband, I am the co-creator of the television magazine, *This Is Baltimore, Too*.

None of this happened overnight, but it happened. I turned my passion into purpose. How? Because I understand what assistant director, Max Radbill, stated our last day on the set of *Water In A Broken Glass*. Speaking to the film's talented writer and director, Jamelle Williams-Thomas, Max said, "Your dreams don't happen unless you make them happen." My dream happened because I dared to dream about becoming a published author in the first place. My dream happened because my parents instilled that confidence in me way back when my mother said, "Well, write, baby," and my father smiled. My dream happened because instead of announcing it to my parents, I proclaimed it to myself then went out and did everything I needed to do to make it happen. And that dream took my passion beyond my wildest dreams.

Chrita Paulin has also dared to dream, and has faced many challenges while trying to make her wildest dreams come true. But knowing that "your dreams don't happen unless you make them happen," Chrita put herself on a course to make her dreams a reality, and as a result, she has received the rewards of turning her passion into purpose. And Chrita wants to help others do the same, which is why she compiled this anthology.

Chrita asked Althea Bates, S. Marie Vargas, Yashate Pendergrass, and Jessica Mayor to share their incredible journeys of how they were fortunate enough to turn their passion into purpose. Through the inspirational testimonies of these phenomenal women, fires will be lit inside people that fear and doubt will not be able to extinguish. After reading the courageous stories in this book, anyone who has a dream of turning their passion into purpose will stare at the words as I stared at the words of that short story when I was a little girl, and proclaim to themselves, "Hey! I wanna do that." And know that they can.

Talk with you soon.

Sincerely,

Odessa Rose

# Odessa Rose

ODESSA ROSE received her B.A. in English from Coppin State University and her M.A. in Literature from the University of Maryland at College Park. She is a recipient of the Just About Books Annual Book Award. Her first novel, *Water In A Broken Glass*, captured the #6 spot on the On-Demand Best Seller list, is ranked #17 on Accredited Online Colleges' 20 Essential Novels For African-American Women list, was recorded for the Maryland School for the Blind, is included in *The Greenwood Encyclopedia of Multiethnic American Literature, Ethnic American Literature: An Encyclopedia for Students,* and *Black Like Us: A Century of Lesbian, Gay, and Bisexual African American Fiction. Water In A Broken Glass* is now a feature film of the same title. Her second novel, *In the Mirror* received the African American Expo Award for Fiction. Rose is a member of the Black Writers Guild of Maryland. She is also the co-creator of the television magazine, *This Is Baltimore, Too.* She resides in her hometown of Baltimore with her husband and three children.

http://odessarose.com/
https://www.facebook.com/odessa.rose.3
https://twitter.com/Odessarose6
https://www.smashwords.com/books/view/454169

# Preface

As a publisher and one who enjoys connecting with the human spirit, I have met so many amazing women who have persevered through love, heart ache, abuse, handicaps, single-parenthood, and more. Despite the difficulties these ladies were confronted with, their stories of survival, determination, and success were even more compelling.

As a young woman, I watched my mother raise my siblings and me as a single parent. She worked excessive hours as a manager of a toy store, but in doing so, she birthed a community of diverse, successful people. My mother dedicated her life to uplifting others through mentorship, friendship, and hard love. Somehow, she made it look so easy I took for granted the pure sacrifices she had to make. The success that my siblings and I have acquired, where made possible by my mother's years of hardship, endurance, and determination to never quit. She would always tell me, "I will shovel shit off of a mule train if it is what I have to do to take care of you all." That was real.

The ladies that have come together to write this book are much like my mother. Circumstances, situations, and people made them feel like giving up. People were counting them out. What people often forget, however, is the power of the human spirit is unstoppable. When a woman has had enough of anything, she will make a way to move that thing out of her path. When a woman makes up her mind to let a person go, although it may be the toughest decision she will make, she will let them go and never look back. When a woman makes up her mind to do anything, you better take notice.

I am giving notice to everyone, authors Althea Bates, S. Marie Vargas, Yashate' Pendergrass, Jessica Mayor, Odessa Rose, and myself, Chrita Paulin, have been forged through fire and are buffing off our shine. We are all, finally, using our passion to walk in our purpose and it feels good.

Join each author on their journey as they share with you how they found the strength to look fear and defeat in the face, and find the passionate, purposeful woman they were created to be.

**Chrita Paulin**
Passion to Purpose Collaborator
President, Coal Under Pressure, LLC

# Acknowledgments

I want to thank all of the fortitudinous women who have taught me everything I know about being a woman. To the women who have sacrificed their own dreams to be phenomenal wives, mothers, sisters, and friends, I thank you.

To my mom, Virginia Taylor: There is never a day that goes by that I do not think about you. You are engrained in my soul. Everything I am, and everything I will be, is because of the sacrifices you have made for me. I pray that you know, you were always the wind beneath my wings.

To the women of Archer, George, and Alice Ann Streets: You are the matriarchs of a generation of remarkable people. Your long hours at work, tireless hours of cooking and cleaning, miles of footsteps to get groceries or to get your children to an event, didn't go unnoticed. I noticed. I watched each of you willingly give up your dreams to raise your children, and in turn, you raised all of us. We were a community, we were a family, we were historical Black Bel Air. Each one of you phenomenal women have left a piece of yourself with me and for that I am honored.

To my high school English Teacher, Doris Williams, for making me memorize, and repeat, *Invictus* by William Ernest Henley. I am truly the master of my fate and the captain of my soul.

To my children, I thank you for inspiring me each and every day of my life. I can't even begin to say how proud I am of each of you. Your lives haven't always been easy, yet you continued to aspire for excellence. You have accomplished so much and I am sure, the best is yet to come. Each and every day you make me laugh. I thank you for the one billion roasts, the jokes that straddle the line, the midnight dance parties, and the nights where there were way too many of you in my bed. It is because of you that I will never stop pursuing my dreams...my dreams of leaving you a legacy you can be proud of and will tell your children over and over again, until they just say, "Enough already!"

To the women of the Passion to Purpose collaboration: Althea, Stephanie, Yashate', and Jessica, you inspire me! You ladies are determined to take your past troubles and turn them to triumphs. You are strong, dedicated, loving individuals with so much to offer the world. I hope this book is just one of many. Continue to share your knowledge with others and be the catalyst others need to press through. Thank you for allowing me to lead you on this journey.

# Chapter One

## JACKIE OF ALL TRADES: MISTRESS OF NONE

### By Chrita Paulin

I was a jack of all trades and a mistress (the feminine word for "master") of none. In retrospect, that is not totally true. I was a mistress...a mistress of quitting everything I started to avoid failure. To understand why I was a master of quitting, and how owning this title impacted my life for years, I must explain how I got there in the first place.

My mother was one of the matriarchs of my community. Back in the 70's, she was one of the only African-American business women in the community I grew up in, managing the largest toy store in the area. My mother was quite impressive. Looking back, I now recognize my mother harnessed diversity and conflict resolution skills far before they became corporate jargon. She hired people of all races, ages, sizes, nationalities. Her motto was, "Everyone started with an A with her". She accepted all people at face value and you would really have to mess up to get on her bad side. Community leaders, law enforcement, and others respected her for her fairness, strength, and determination to provide a good life for her children. Like I said, she was quite impressive.

Being my mother's daughter, however, was both a blessing and a curse. Because my mother worked at the toy store, I was able to learn unique skills at a very young age such as chess, how to play the violin, how to paint, how to make an authentic cheesecake, I witnessed an authentic Hindi wedding, and was a special guest at the release of Dorothy Hamill's Ice Skating shows (for those of you who are old enough to remember), and more. The employees respected my mother's management style and, in turn, were more than willing to entertain me and teach me things during the many hours I spent in the store.

One thing I always enjoyed was listening to the people tell me about my mom. They would often tell me about how they met her, why she hired them, how she helped them in their time of need, how they confided in her...you get the picture. I loved the fact that everyone thought my mother was such a great person, but after a while I started noticing a pattern. Not only where the people in awe of my mother, they "just knew" her children were going to grow up and be amazing also! Despite my mother being a single mother at a time when divorce was not common, everyone believed, Virginia Taylor's children were going to grow up and be someone important.

Over the years, the praise, at least for me, began to feel like pressure. I am sure I did it to myself, but I began to feel like everyone was expecting me to be as phenomenal as my mother. I fell into my own trap. I put the pressure on myself to excel at everything. And tragically, this is when my fear of failure began. In my mind, if I failed at anything I would let my mother down or ruin her reputation in the community. I couldn't chance it.

I knew what I had to do. I had to avoid failure by any means necessary. The plan was easy. I either didn't try anything I knew I couldn't do, or I would quit anything I tried the moment I suspected failure was inevitable. Violin, dance, modeling, medical school, law school, all became victims of my fear of failure. I have had too many opportunities to count that I have given up on, rather than people being able to see me not succeed. I believed my plan was brilliant and had even convinced myself that I was very successful. I graduated college, I had a prosperous career with the federal government, I had just gotten married, and was starting my family. It wasn't until I wanted to leave my job to be a full-time mother that I began to question my future. What would I do with myself as a stay-at-home mom? How would I occupy my time? What could I do to contribute to my household, financially?

### You Failed, So What?

I pondered my decision to leave the workplace for months. The stress of worrying about losing my income, raising a family full time, and not knowing what I would do in the future was killing me. I talked to friends and family and received mixed feelings causing me more anxiety. The majority thought I was crazy to give up such a lucrative salary, though no one really understood how badly I wanted to be a stay-at-home mommy. In my heart I knew what I wanted to do but the fear of such a life-change was daunting. I would have never suspected my decision and confirmation would be found in a book store.

Every Friday night my husband and I would have a date at the local book store. This particular Friday, I was a little down because I knew my time to make a decision was approaching. We found a table in the café, I ordered a mocha coffee, and began talking about my fears. I was afraid of making the wrong decision, l was afraid of being a bad mom, I was afraid of what people would say…I was afraid of failure. Despite my husband's support and reassurance, I still couldn't overcome the fear and doubt in my head. As we were talking, however, I received, what I considered, "a sign from God". As I was repeating in my head, "God please tell me what I need to do," I looked up and right in front of me was a magazine with the title that read, "You Fail, So What!" Let me say it again, it read, "You Fail, So What!".

I was mesmerized by God's awesomeness, and His never-ending ability to make the resolutions to the problems in my life so simplistic. In that moment I realized my God knew my problems all along and was simply waiting on me to ask Him for the resolution. He showed me my questions were not about what I wanted to do, if I was going to be a good mother or not, or how we would make it on one income. God showed me my issue was purely fear. The fear of failure had loomed in my life once again and had me second guessing what I wanted to do all along. I wanted to be a stay-at-home mother, until my children were able to walk and talk, at least that's what I told myself. So without further hesitation, I submitted my resignation and made plans to be the storybook wife and mother, just like the fairytale dreams most little girls my age had.

## Please! No More Dora the Explorer

When my first daughter was born, I tried to be the perfect mother. I took her to the park, put my daughter in every activity I could, found the best starter schools, and so on. After my second and third child, I started to feel guilty because, although I loved my children, I needed that intellectual banter that I missed from adulting. You know, the debating over a project, the news, anything that required you to use your intellectual ability. Watching Dora the Explorer every day helped me realize you always needed a map, a plan, but the song was emblazoned in my head, the repeated episodes in my mind,

I began to realize that I did not truly understand all that I had given up, being a stay-at-home. I remember calling my sister (who was also a stay-at-home mom), ranting about the fact I no longer made my own money, or had an adult to talk to during the day. I went on about how I missed challenging projects and dressing up. My sister patiently listened, releasing a little laugh here and there, until I had finished venting all of my pent-up frustration which was clearly more than I realized. After I finished, my sister said, "You should write about this. You should share this with other mothers who are going through the same thing."

She was right. I needed an outlet. I decided it was time to go back to doing the one thing I truly loved all my life...writing. I decided I was going to start a newsletter for professional women, like me, who had left the corporate world to raise their children. Not that I have anything against other stay-at-home moms, I just wanted to write a letter that addressed women like me, ones who had given up lucrative, well-paying careers, to raise their family and the challenges they faced.

For the premier issue, I found contributing authors who wrote about everything from the challenges they faced, to the societal stereotypes of being a stay-at-home dad. The newsletter was so good, my mailing list went from the anticipated 25 women to well over 150 women. I had found my at-home niche, that intellectual tantalization I had been missing for months. The newsletter was so good, my sister and others recommended I sent a copy of the newsletter to Oprah, who was the hottest talk show host in the business (an arguably is still so today). As a writer, I knew you never sent unsolicited manuscripts to television shows, but I got caught up in all the excitement. I addressed the envelope and handed it to the mailman the next day.

I waited, believing that Oprah was going to call me and tell me how fantastic the newsletter was and that I had truly stumbled upon a topic that was relevant to society. I never heard from Oprah. Instead, I received what I have considered both a blessing and a kick in the gut.

A month or so after I submitted the newsletter I was sitting at the kitchen table watching Oprah when nausea began to consume me. I sat and watched as Oprah did her first show on stay-at-home parents, not just any parents, but people who left the corporate world to raise their children. Yes, everything I had put into that newsletter, every article people had written, was discussed in that show. What hurt even worse, the show was so successful, it was at that point Oprah started doing "Oprah After the Show". The topics on the show was so intense, she couldn't finish the discussion in the hour provided, so she finished the rest of the segment in "Oprah's After the Show". I will not lie, it took me a minute to get over this. Amidst people telling me I should try to contact Oprah or I should sue, I knew this was my mistake. I knew not to send unsolicited materials but I got caught up, I felt like I failed, and I used this incident as an excuse to bring "Jackie" out to play.

### Safe Doesn't Mean Successful

Over the next years of my life I operated in "safe mode". Just like a computer in "safe mode" where extra precautions are taken to prevent the computer from getting a virus, I took every effort to make sure anything I engaged in was fail proof. Despite the plethora of opportunities offered me, I would always take the easy way out. I appeared very successful, but was I really? Is one truly successful if they never challenge themselves? Is one truly successful if they allow the fear of failure to keep them from their dreams, goals, or aspirations? Absolutely not. Over time, I recognized what I was doing and I became resentful. I became resentful that I gave up on myself. I allowed my fear of public opinion pave my life's journey for way too many years. I was that "Jackie", until I wasn't.

## My Tipping Point

Fear will have you lying to yourself. You manage to rationalize your excuses, and tell yourself lies when your fears become bigger than your willingness to fight for your dreams. I had become great at lying to myself. "I can't take that job because my children will not be able to function if I am not home." "I can't start that business because it will take too much time from the family." "I can't write that book because there are people who might not like what I write or may be offended." You get the picture. The funny thing, the very people I used for my excuses not to do things, are the very ones that pushed me to my tipping point. I knew what I was doing, and my family did, too. My husband would continually tell me I needed to take a chance, step out on faith and go for my dreams. Although his support encouraged me, it was my children that tipped me. You see, as I was passing up opportunities, being cautious, letting fear get in the way, my children were labeling me as someone who was "scared" and "made excuses" instead of doing what I wanted to do. I believed my children saw me as successful, instead they saw me as "'safe". They knew my dreams. They knew what I was fully capable of, but they never saw me make it happen.

I felt like a failure with my children. My attempts to avoid looking like a failure, resulted in me feeling like a failure to the people I loved the most. It was a journey, but my tipping point had come. I was either going to continue operating out of fear of failure and never realize my dreams, or I was going to do me, unapologetically. I chose the latter.

## How to Remove Fear and Be the Best You

Fear will consume you. If you are operating out of fear, I am sure you already know it. I can imagine you often resent yourself for playing it safe, instead of going for that one thing you truly want. Been there, done that. I am here to tell you, you do not have to continue operating in fear. You do not have to continue playing it "safe". You can be fearless, unapologetic, but it takes work and time.
Here are some concrete steps you can use to start on your journey of removing fear, and finding your purpose:

1. With social media, your efforts are often out there for people to see, and they do not hesitate to call you out. Do not let yourself get caught in "safe" mode on the internet. Recognize that everyone has an opinion. It is up to you to determine what information you allow to consume your mental space. If you see a comment starts getting negative, do not read it. Move on to the next message. Alternatively, on business pages, remove the ability for others to comment. It is up to you to protect your social media space. Most importantly, do not post negative messages if you do not want negativity back.
2. Write down a list of your goals. Identify the reasons you feel you are not able to complete the goals. Then go down the list again, critically, truly assessing if what you wrote is a reason or an excuse. Eliminate the excuses from your mind.
3. Push yourself a little every day. Most people have a fear of going out of their comfort zone. It's normal. Those who are truly successful, however, never stay within their comfort zone. Truly successful people challenge themselves every day, seeking new opportunities to push themselves to the limit. I am not advocating for risky or dangerous behavior. Rather, I am encouraging you to push yourself intellectually, mentally, and creatively. I am

encouraging you to understand your boundaries and then exploring the opportunities outside those boundaries that may catapult you towards your dreams, goals, and purpose.
4. Recognize that fear is not in your DNA. Humans are given are certain DNA structure that creates the way they look, how many fingers they have, if they can curl their tongue, and so on. DNA does not give a person fear. Although some scientists have suggested fear is innate, just like one's natural fight or flight instinct, fear can be controlled and/or eliminated. It is a mental state that you control. Make a choice to not be fearful and work towards it. Remember it is not in your DNA, you are not stuck with fear forever.
5. Talk to yourself! Tell yourself each day, "I am not fearful". "I will do what it takes to achieve my dreams and fear cannot stop me." "Fear is not in my DNA. It is in my mind. My mind tells me to be bold, brave, courageous, unapologetic, in the pursuit of my goals, dreams, and purpose."
6. Turn your "fear" into "F.E.A.R". Throw your old understanding of fear away. It's time to change the way you look at and define fear. Instead of saying I operate in fear, say I operate in "F.E.A.R". You have the FREEDOM to do what you want to do. You will ENGAGE in opportunities and purpose know that you will succeed. You will ACKNOWLEDGE both your successes and failures with optimism. And lastly, you will RISE to meet the person you were truly meant to be.

You have the power to determine who you want to be and how successful you want to be. Whether it be fear of failure, fear of success, or some other fear, it is time to change your mindset.

"Keep the body strong. Take the mind," --
Denzel Washington discussing Willie Lynche's method of keeping people enslaved in the movie, "The great Debaters".

My final words to you...Watch who you allow to consume your mind. People spend multiple hours each day on social media trying to impress others, worrying about how many likes they get on their posts, and taking in comments people make about you. Don't be "enslaved". Don't be of strong body and let others control your mind. This includes your business.

If you have a vision and you know the purpose of your business, do you really need others to validate what you are doing? Move in your purpose, without fear, and be of strong mind. Protect your mind and intellectual space like you protect your children, your cars, your homes.

Be fearless from this day forward and go for all your dreams, visions, and goals that you long thought were unattainable. You can do it! I look forward to hearing your praise report.

# Chrita Paulin

Chrita Paulin is the owner and President of Coal Under Pressure, LLC. After a successful thirteen year career with the Department of Defense, Chrita took on the career of her life...motherhood. Chrita's desire to stay at home with her children and to utilize her entrepreneurial skills, led her to publish the Antares Chronicles, a bi-weekly newsletter dedicated to women and men who left corporate careers to become stay-at-home parents. The overwhelming success of the Antares Chronicles sparked Chrita to begin her freelance writing career. In 2004, she created Coal Under Pressure as a publishing company for freelance and independent writers.

Since that time, Chrita has written for numerous magazines, blogs, and educational institutions. Through Coal Under Pressure, Chrita has launched the careers of authors in the poetry, fiction, religious studies, auto biographical, and self-help genres. She also pitched, marketed, and acquired funding for various film projects. In addition to publishing, Chrita is a Managing partner of Distorted eSports, LLC and the Antares Mall. She is an Adjunct Professor, a Court-appointed Guardian Ad Litem, and a women's coach and mentor, teaching women to "Stretch In". In her latest pursuit, Chrita launched "Perceptual Distortions," a podcast focused on practical conflict management and resolution strategies everyone can use.

She lives with her husband of twenty-two years and five beautiful children in the sunny state of Florida.

She is the author of Let's Bake a Family, Just What I Needed to Hear: The Writer's Guide to Removing Fear, Doubt, and the Angst of Failure, The Five Steps to Family: A five-step approach to finding your biological parents, a chapter in Letters to My Father, and Historical Black Bel Air.

Pleas e feel free to contact me at any time at :

- www.coalunderpressure.com
- Coal underpressurepubs@gmail.com
- Facebook: @coalunderpressurellc
- Twitter: @cup_publishing
- Instagrarm: @coalunderpressure

# Chapter 2

## BROKENNESS, BAGGAGE, AND BLESSINGS

### By Althea Bates

Brokenness, Baggage, and Blessings served as the backdrop to my life story. A story of happiness, hurt, growth, pain, anger, fear, boldness, and resiliency. A life documented, lived, and survived. I am a survivor. I have not only survived, I have thrived on my journey to becoming Althea Webber Bates. I am still learning and being molded into the best version of myself. My sharing what I have learned so far on the journey to becoming me is with the intent that I may inspire someone else.

Looking back now, I can clearly see how I transitioned through the phases of my life. While going through, it is hard, seemingly impossible, to see your way out of it. For me, I had to go through brokenness and baggage before I could see my blessings manifest themselves in my life. Brokenness describes the time when I was falling to pieces and living a shell of an existence. Baggage represents the weight that I carried from the broken pieces, some my own and some baggage of others I picked up along the way. Blessings describe the results of my learning the process, of allowing God to mend the broken pieces, and of my letting go of the baggage to allow myself to experience the blessings.

## Brokenness

Brokenness is the very act of watching your life fall to pieces; a condition usually evoked and shaped by the experiences we encounter throughout our lives. Looking back at my life: sexual abuse survivor, married young, divorced, child out of wedlock, abortion, failed relationships and two broken legs, etc., all played a role in my life spiraling out of control. My life story had all the makings of a Lifetime Movie but this was no movie, in fact, this was real life staring me in the face. All this, and I hadn't even reached my 30th birthday. Sometimes I feel like I am having an out of body experience when I think of all the things I have been through. I mean how does this happen to someone like me, someone with goals, hopes, dreams and a vision for their life? To tell you the truth, it's easier than you think. Once I took my eyes off God and his plan for my life things started to spiral out of control. The truth is, I was so busy trying to appear to have it all together so no one could see my broken pieces that I missed all the warning signs. I was too busy hiding behind the mask to see what was right in front of me.

Masks are real. We use masks to hide behind, to protect ourselves, or even to host the characters, the facade, we have created to keep folks from seeing who we really are! I learned, and became, an expert at compartmentalizing my brokenness. I could create a mask to hide behind for virtually every situation in my life. I was the smart girl. People called me smart and I eagerly embraced it. I hid behind that labeling because it was safe. As long as everyone was looking at how smart I was, I believed no one would question my broken pieces. To tell you the truth, I spent so much time trying to develop a personality I could safely hide behind that it took me years to find myself again.

Whoever said it was unimportant for a dad to be in a little girl's life, they were not telling the truth. My dad was everything to me. Having experienced abuse at a young age by a family friend, I realized that my dad was the center of my universe, as well as, my sense of safety. I grew up in Jamaica. My dad was present in my life but he did not ever live with us. He had his own family to go home to at night. My parents had an affair and, of course, I was the product of that affair. When I learned how I was conceived, I always felt a heavy burden of guilt for changing the course of my parents' life forever. Although both my parents never made me feel this in the way they loved or cared for me, it was still something I felt personally responsible for.

At the age of nine, my world was severed. My mom announced that we would be migrating to America to live with my aunt in Connecticut and, of course, my dad wouldn't be going with us. This was the hardest part of leaving and coming to the United States. We came to America with the dreams and hopes my mom had for a better future. The excitement of living with her sister, however, quickly faded to disappointment. The turmoil between my mother and her sister was difficult and I began to retreat into myself, becoming more introverted than I already was. My mom was working two jobs trying to make ends meet so we could move of out of my aunt's house. I felt I had no control and I continued to retreat into my own cocoon as my sense of normalcy and safety net had all been taken away.

Growing up I continued to be introverted and was considered a "good girl" by my mother and others. I was a tomboy for sure and didn't have much interest in traditional girl related activities. I wanted to play video games, climb trees, ride bikes, etc., nevertheless, I hid behind the good girl mask. It was easy to play the part of the "good girl" because I was super shy and people just made the correlation. I grew up in a predominantly West Indian Pentecostal Church. Not having a connection or contact with my parents' family the members of the church became our family. Despite the love and warmth, the church members showed me, I remember feeling alone. I felt God couldn't possibly love me, especially because of the way I was conceived. I literally thought God couldn't bless the mess. Thinking back, I wasn't ready to let go of that burden I was carrying and let God do the work in my life.

## Baggage

The baggage people carry can come in many forms. For some the baggage is filled with relationship hurt, for some it might be financial hurt, and for others it might even be church hurt. I carried my parents' baggage although it was not my burden to bear since learning at six years old how I was conceived. After begging my parents to tell me truth about their relationship I carried that guilt and shame with me and wore it as a badge of honor. I remember even thinking the things that would happen to me in my future would be deserved punishment for the sin that I represented in being born. The guilt and baggage of my parents, along with the sexual abuse I experienced, influenced my life in so many ways. I went from being a super outgoing, vibrant child to being withdrawn and reserved. I remember my mom taking me to see a doctor a couple times a week, in an attempt to find out what was wrong with me. I felt like I needed to protect her and so I made the decision that I would not share with her my feelings or what had happened to me until I was thirteen. My thought process was that I would be mature enough to have a conversation with her and that, by then, some distance would have passed since the abuse. By then, I believed, she wouldn't do something that could send her to prison and take her away from me. Knowing my mother's temperament back then, I wasn't willing to take the chance.

So on my 13th birthday I had one of the hardest conversations any child my age would ever have with a parent. I told my mom about the sexual abuse I had endured and talked with her about the guilt I felt because of her and my dad's affair. During that time of my life I remember having feelings of being alone, of desperation, of fear. I was also being bullied on my ride on the school bus from the city where we lived to a suburban school daily. I was the joke and recipient of teasing, taunts, and having things thrown at me for the duration of each bus ride. I left this school after four years and went back to school in the city.

I can remember having conversations with myself and telling myself that when I grew up I didn't want to get married, I didn't want to have kids, and I didn't want to have a family. I just wanted to focus on my career and didn't need to be with anyone because they would get in the way of my education and career. While my friends had all these hopes and dreams which included all of these things mentioned, I was busy trying to figure out how I could avoid and void them from my life.

I created a life plan for myself that was based on accomplishing personal/professional, as well as, education and career advancement related goals. My ex-husband came along during my senior year of high school. He was funny, he made me laugh, he was fascinated by my "good girl" persona, and our friendship grew into us dating by the time college came around. We went to college together for the first two years before I transferred to school out of state. Maintaining a long-distance relationship was hard on both of us. During my junior year of college, I got pregnant and we made the decision to have an abortion. This went against everything I believed in but I was not prepared to be anyone's mother, not by any means. By my senior year of college, I felt like I wanted to see what being single was like. After having a boyfriend all the way through college, I just wanted a change. We broke up for a couple months of my senior year and before the close of that year I remember feeling like I was finally on the verge of discovering myself. Needless to say, the proposal definitely took me by surprise. In hindsight, I was young and was not ready for marriage and neither was he, at least not with me. We had been together for years. He was comfortable, he was familiar, which made it easy to say, "Yes, I'll marry you". I had no idea and no clue what marriage meant. My parents didn't provide me with a traditional example of marriage. I was 24 and in love with idea of marriage but not necessarily in love with the person I was marrying.

At 25 I was married, scared, depressed, and broken. Needless to say, our marriage didn't last long. We had gotten married for all the wrong reasons in the first place. By 26 I was a young divorcee and had moved back in with my mom. During this time, I distanced myself from everyone. I needed time and space to heal, to process my feelings, and emotions. After a while I started to create new friendships but was still very guarded and cautious. A year later, at the age of 27, I conceived my son out of wedlock, while in the church. This trial was one of hardest experiences I would endure as I was isolated, lonely, and afraid. I decided to focus my energies on raising my son and on my education and career advancement. Three months after giving birth to my son I started Graduate School to pursue my Master's Degree in Human Services.

## Blessings

So many things have happened and so many transitions have taken place over the course of my young life. From the ages of 9-13 we moved a total of five times with my mom's goal of moving us to a better neighborhood. During that time, I had several mentors that I became connected with in elementary and high school. I now know God placed them in my life at the intricate times that I needed each of them. I appreciate now the sacrifices my mom made to put food on the table and to make sure we had an adequate roof over our heads. Back then, however, I did not display or feel the same level of gratitude. I resented her for so many reasons and punished her with my silence and passive aggressive behavior. I unknowingly was trying to make her pay for having to be transplanted to the US, having to leave my Dad behind, and then having to watch her struggle to get back to the same quality of life, if not better, than what we left behind in Jamaica.

Moving into adulthood was not an easy time for me but I received many blessings despite my brokenness and my baggage. Transitioning from college, to marriage, to divorce, to being a single parent, were major life changes. It's hard to find the blessings when your life includes so many twists as turns but then again that's life. You never know what life has around the bend. I am recalling my life story and thinking about the exact moment in time that I considered my life a blessing. I think I would have to say that wasn't until I had my son at the age of 27. I remember feeling and imagining what my mom must have felt having me at around the same age. I felt blessed to bring a child into this world, blessed to experience being a mother (especially for someone who grew up not wanting to have children or a family).

For me so much began and ended with the birth of my son. After having my son, I felt fueled to go after my dreams and goals in life. I had a reason to prove myself and make something of my life. I started my Master's Degree Program when my son was three months (with the support of my Mom and My Son's Father) and never looked back. I was motivated to make something better of my life for him. I got my Master's Degree, received a promotion, bought a home, and launched a consulting business, all in the preceding four years following the birth of my son. Life was on an upward trajectory for me. I felt the blessings were rolling in. I got offered an adjunct professor job at a local college and launched my consultant business doing training and professional development for nonprofits. I was living the dream, or so I thought.

I finally thought that life was dealing me a blessed hand. At 33, I had all the things I thought I needed and most of the things that I wanted had manifested in my life. So, getting ready to experience a life altering circumstance such as breaking two legs five months apart (one on black ice, the other on marble floors balancing on one crutch) was the farthest thing from my mind. Going through rehabilitation and learning how to walk again was one of the most excruciating and painful things I have gone through to date. Out of work for almost a year due to the leg injury gave me loads of time to think, process, meditate, pray, and write. Once you experience a situation that changes your life, causing you to assess your life, you can't look at life the same way again. Being alive is a blessing, in its own right.

After that year I vowed to live a life of intention and impact. My perspective related to understanding brokenness and baggage and what it meant to be resilient over these obstacles, challenges, and circumstances in my life gained new found clarity. I began to grasp the concept and importance of birthing my purpose. By 35 I started dating and then married my husband. I had my second child, my daughter, and just started Doctoral School. I was focused on my life goals moving toward to my dissertation process and then attained a new job as a director at a local nonprofit. I was on a trajectory moving towards accomplishing my dreams. In 2016, God reminded me of our conversations during the time I had broken my leg in 2009. He had spoken to me about Resiliency and then shared that it was time to launch the work he gave me in supporting women with their resiliency.

In 2016, I launched Project Resiliency Movement, a social movement to empower and encourage women in areas of resiliency and self-care. What an amazing journey it has been since launching this organization. So many additional blessings have been gained along this path: launching conferences, speaking at events, writing books, developing partnerships and collaborations. I don't know what the future holds for me but I can say that it is a bright one full of abundant blessings.

## Conclusion

A life unexplored is definitely a life not worth living. I can truly say thus far I have lived, loved, and survived. I love and respect all the aspects of my brokenness, baggage and blessings because I would not be me without any of the experiences, paths, or journeys explored throughout my life. The journey to finding myself has been one that I would not change because it has molded and shaped me into the best version of myself. If I were to give my younger self any advice it would be to not live a life based on fear, but to explore your life and your path in spite of the fear you might feel in that moment. Moments make up a lifetime of memories. Although some memories might be good, bad, or indifferent, they are all worth exploring to meet you where you are. I have learned that I am where I am supposed to be in my own journey to living a resilient lifestyle. I hope, trust and pray that this life chapter and book inspires you to live your best life journey, one that is fully explored. As you begin your journey, please consider the following:

1. **Birthing Purpose Requires Self-Discipline.** I learned the hard way that you cannot hold on to old "stuff" and baggage and expect to birth purpose. These two things cannot co-exist in the same space. You must let go of the past: past hurt, disappointments, and failures, to tap into our purpose.

What are you willing to do for that dream? I heard Will Smith recently state, "Self-discipline is at the center of all success." How many of us lack self-discipline? It starts with your mindset. Is your mindset tuned into a winning frequency? Are you self-disciplined enough to not sabotage your own success?

2. **Intentionality in Favor.** I recently heard a speech given by Iyanla Vanzant in which she discussed intentions. Everything we do is intentional and our intentionality influences our potential and purpose. You go to sleep with intention; you wake up with intention; you gossip with intention; you waste time with intention; you ignore your purpose with intention. Intentionality is in everything we do whether we want to admit it or not. We are intended to do something, to leave a mark or a footprint. How do you go about using your intentionality? Do you use your intentionality to speak positive affirmations over your life and others? Do you use your intentionality to go after opportunities instead of waiting for them to be dropped in your lap? My Bible says seek and ye shall find. Are you seeking with intentionality?

Are you praying with intentionality? Are you specifically seeking God out asking him to reveal the how, the when, and the why? The issue with many of us is we do not connect the dots. We seek certain things and when those things come, we reject it, waiting for it to come in the specific package which we have envisioned. Intentionality doesn't come wrapped in a nice beautiful bow, intentionality takes grunt, roll up your sleeves, work. Are you willing to roll up your sleeves and get dirty for your vision? Are you willing to sacrifice for your vision, go without, and/or give up things for your vision? If you are not willing to make the sacrifices then do not bother going after it? When the visionary is ready, the vision will align itself, but not without sacrifice and intentionality.

3. **Shifting Your Alignment to His Assignment.** Sarah Jakes Roberts states, "my attention is an investment". You can't attach yourself to things and people in this season of Vision Casting that devalues your investment. God has allowed me to see I was self-disciplined, I had a vision-aligned mindset, I leaped and took risks to get to the reward

on the other end, I was intentional making my vision a priority, and lastly, I out believed everyone else around me. You must protect the vision at all costs. It is yours to carry, it is yours to bear, and it is yours to birth.

Shifting my alignment to his assignment begs the following questions. Are you on your grind? What does your grind look like? Are you grinding, planting those seeds to be fruitful in time? Are your devouring and attacking your vision? What are you telling and speaking to your vision and over your life? Nothing beats a try but a failure. Are you throwing your whole self at the vision? If the vision doesn't turn out to be your thing, then it was your lesson and pathway necessary to that vision. Be consistent in your pursuits of your vision. The right collaborators/ partners will align themselves with you based on your diligence and consistency. What are you willing to leave behind in pursuits of your vision? You cannot take everyone and everything with you where you are going? You must hold on to the vision in one hand and let go of the things you do not need to take with you to pursue the vision in the other hand?

The truth is everyone needs resilience. This is what allows us to overcome adversities in our everyday lives. It is what we do when we incur life's major setbacks, such as losing a job, a failed relationship, financial loss, as well as, health-related issues that is the true test of our resiliency. Activating and increasing our resiliency muscles allows us to address obstacles that may come our way.

Whether you are aware of it or not, all people keep a running account of what is happening to them, what it means, and what they should do. In other words, our minds are constantly monitoring and interpreting. That is just how we stay on track. But sometimes the interpretation process goes awry. Some people put more extreme interpretations on things that happen—and then react with exaggerated feelings of anxiety, depression, anger, or superiority. Mindsets frame the running account that's taking place in people's heads. They guide the whole interpretation process. The fixed mindset creates an internal monologue that is focused on judging. Realign your mindset so you can focus on your success.

# Althea Bates

"When you live in your purpose, you find little time to dwell in your past"

For over 18 years Althea Bates has worked in social services and workforce development. Growing up in a strong Jamaican family that always encouraged her to dream and work hard Althea has found her way to becoming more than she had initially set her eyes onto. She has found herself functioning as an Entrepreneur, a Professor/Lecturer, a Nonprofit Leader, Directors for various organizations and most recently an author and a Champion for women empowerment issues. Within her educational pursuits she has received a Bachelor's of Science in Psychology from Temple University, Masters of Science from Springfield College in Human Services with a concentration in Organizational Management and Leadership and is currently a Doctoral Candidate at Capella University.

Ms. Webber-Bates currently operates as the CEO and Founder of A. Bates Consulting which provides a range of training -related consulting services to nonprofits/municipalities relative to topics and areas in youth development, case management, workforce development and human services practices. In August of 2016,

Althea launched and founded The Project Resiliency Movement and kicked it off with the #Resilience Conference in 2016 which hosted over 250 women of all backgrounds supporting each other through workshop and interactive activities while women embraced the fact that they don't always have to be strong. This conference opened the path for a 2nd conference entitled Destination Resiliency which inspired the writing of "Destination Resiliency: A Self-Care Planner and Guide (2017) which has reached over 300 people since its initial printing. The theme for both events came from Mrs. Bates belief that "we can as women of color uplift each other consistently, because supporting my sister in her time of need provides healing and resiliency to both of us."

As these women empowerment programs continued to enhance those around her and the connections to women she gained seemed to evolve, Project Resiliency was born. Project Resiliency has become a social movement that seeks to encourage and empower women of color in areas of self-care and resilience related to mental, physical and emotional health while providing connectivity and supports to other women of color through resilience circles (organic meetups in a local park), conferences, workshops and summer seminars. This also highlighted that women wanted to remain connected for longer than just the moment. Watching true relationships bloom in others motivated Althea's own desire to write her own stories; to heal others, as she healed herself.

Althea Webber-Bates continued her work as an author & co-author putting put book projects including: Favor in Failure (2018); Life Balance for the Women on the Rise (2017) and Soaring into Greatness (2017) as well as Brokenness, Baggage and Blessings (2018). In finding her voice and owning her journey she also found in herself the gift of presenting high energy messages that takes the audience through her own personal journey and the purpose she found as she built her Resiliency. Throughout her years as a motivational speaker and author Althea relates to teens, adults and corporations alike inspiring and motivating them to begin the process of healing through empowerment.

Today Althea seeks to facilitate personal and professional growth while motivating her audience to find their resilience personally and professionally using their narratives to facilitate the path to success. While inspiring others professionally she hopes to be inspiring the ones she loves the most her son Zyaan and daughter Sakinah who are the light of her days. She also shares and amazing life with her husband Harry Bates who motivates her to travels widely, read everything, write about her experiences all while they as a family enjoy every moment living in Hartford, CT a community they believe in and commit to healing.

For Booking Information Contact
223 Garden Street, Hartford, CT 06105
Cell: (860) 804-5345
Abatesconsulting@gmail.com

# Chapter 3

## IN THE MIDST OF MY RESISTANCE: DESIGNED ON PURPOSE

### By S. Marie Vargas

**Resistance**: When we fail to accept or comply with something we believe and decide it is not good for us or no longer acceptable. My story is about how I resisted a doctor's diagnosis and positioned myself to research alternative methods of treatment. In turn, this confirmed my true passion and how I recognized my purpose to empower others to learn about preventative health.

I started with the definition of resistance because it is important to be clear about taking a stand for important decisions in our lives. We should not be indifferent when setting our health goals. It's powerful to learn that we own the freedom, as human beings, to resist being blinded by the world.

A quote by Maya Angelou reminds us not to get caught up with the mistakes of our past and affirms that we can only do our best work yet in that moment in time. When I thought about her quote, it transcended a deep and meaningful understanding that it is ok to make mistakes and resist some changes in our lives. It is not ok to expect our lives to change if we keep doing the same mistakes. How do we learn that to make a difference in our lives we have to learn to identify those things preventing us from moving onto our purpose?

I believe fate led you to find this book. I hope the different journeys shared by the women in this book encourage you to turn your passions into your lifelong purpose.

While searching for answers, have you confronted red lights instead of green lights, not finding your expected results? In Pitbull's song *Greenlight*, LunchMoney Lewis sings a piece where he reminds people that we only have one life to live, we should live it up to the fullest, and that there no need to wait to live the live we want to live right now.

I totally agree—we have one life and should live it up! How does one do that when diagnosed with a "lifelong"-crippling condition? Where do you find the strength to continue? Henry Ford said, "When everything seems to be going against you, remember that the airplane takes off against the wind, not with it." Therefore, when responding to challenging situations we must remember there will always be opposition; we cannot let that stop us. How do we do this despite many closed doors and challenges? Did you know your true power lies in having total control of how you respond to any given situation? Should you respond to chaos differently?

If you are questioning how much control you have over unexpected life situations, please know that you have full control of your choices. You own the right of how polite to be when deciding what's best for your life's sake! By knowing you hold the power over your life and won't stay silent about fighting for your wellness, you have allowed courage to master your fears. Mark Twain said it best: Courage is resistance to fear, mastery of fear, not absence of fear. The fear will always be there to distract you, but the power lies in how we control our fears and how we respond to it.

Have you ever resisted, failed to listen, or complied with certain unexpected events in your life? An example is having someone tell you why they think you should not pursue a certain goal or dream you've been having for years. What if you are diagnosed by your doctor without exhausting all available opinions? When presented with events like these, not knowing what direction to take, it can be daunting.

In this book I will emphasize my story of desperation and resistance with the hope to inspire you to continue your journey, knowing you are not alone because caring people have been placed by the creator to get you to your purpose. It's ok to take a stand for your life and tell the world you are no longer moving through the current like a dead fish.

How can you turn your God given talents and passions into your purpose to help those around you? Recently, I came across a short video by Dr. Phil, the TV psychiatrist, talking about how frustrating it is to spend years receiving medication and treatments prescribed by doctors without seeing any results. One piece of advice he gives to his viewers is that it is ok to ask as many questions as you need to your doctor, because at the end of the day it is your precious life and health that is involved. I strongly agreed with Dr. Phil when he mentioned that if you haven't seen any improvement then its ok to go get a second, or perhaps a third, opinion. Despite the fact that I was given a lifelong diagnosis that was set out to cripple me, I did not give up. I was offered a standard medical treatment that had more side effects than positive effects on my health. I refused it. I thought to myself there had to be another option. It is very important for you to know what the side effects of your decisions are going to be and if they will be the best course of action for whatever it is you may be going through.

Do you agree with taking a pharmaceutical drug that will give you more side effects than what it is supposed to help you? I wasn't. It is totally your call because you hold the power to how you want to live your life. On the other hand, you may want to research different approaches that may have fewer side effects and could be less detrimental to your health.

Recently, I watched a documentary called Unrest on Netflix about Jennifer Brea, a woman who was diagnosed with mysterious chronic illness. Jennifer set out to learn the rarity of her disease. Unfortunately, even though she was experiencing pain, along with many other symptoms, doctors kept telling her that there was nothing wrong with her. Thankfully, Jennifer never gave up and she continued to look for other opinions until she finally found an immunologist who was able to help her decipher where her debilitating pain came from.

Jennifer's documentary captures the actual sorrow of what it is to live with a chronic illness and she expresses her growing passion for finding a cure to her mystery illness. My story relates to her so much and it has been empowering to know that I share the same passion as her when it comes to not giving up on finding a better quality of life. To make this documentary, Jennifer reached out to hundreds of other chronic illness sufferers and started a supportive community to bring light to those suffering in silence. Her resistance of not accepting and not giving up on her health has inspired me to continue my journey. Similarly, I have also started a supportive community to bring awareness to alternative options and to motivate and empower others to not quit investigating solutions. If you, or someone you know, are interested in being part of this supportive group, please connect with me via email.

When faced with chaos and undesirable situations, the first thing most people do is give up. For a moment, this was me. Sometime ago, I was diagnosed with Rheumatoid Arthritis and it was one of the most detrimental times. I cried and asked God, "why me?" Soon after, there came a moment when I said, "Enough is enough; I will not settle for belittling myself in the corner." In the middle of my pain, I realized God was not punishing me; he was preparing me for His plan. Then, as hard as it was to wake up every single day, I knew I needed to go out there and find a solution to the exacerbating symptoms crashing down my world before my eyes.

Life has taught me that no matter how cloudy our vision may get, we are in total control of how our goals will be fulfilled. Our state of mind will dictate our actions, which will dictate how hard we work for our success. I forced myself to read uplifting books and scriptures from the bible so that my positive outlook on life remained strong. Ask any chronic illness sufferer to tell you how hard it is to motivate oneself when the pain is overbearing, and nobody understands. It is a bittersweet reality that we are not always going to get to live a preferred life. We must enjoy each morning we are alive. This confirms every day is a gift and full of chances to be of service to others.

In all honesty, I had expected to be done with school by the time I turned thirty. This is not the case. I returned to school to better serve those I am supporting. I've realized I love learning about preventative medicine and enjoy being a lifelong learner. Nonetheless, even though my life hasn't gone according to plan, I recognize I have been blessed and God has not forsaken me, even in the midst of my resistance. My wish for you reading this book, going through a challenging situation, is to remember that your life is full of blessings. Joyfully, I want to affirm that wherever you are in the journey we call life; you are right where you need to be. Yes, you may be going through the motions only to think you are not advancing anywhere in life. Dear friend, please know that there is a reason and it is ok for you not to understand it at this very moment.

We often hear about how success is never a straight-through journey; it takes hard work and dedication to achieve anything in life. Indeed, the work we put in will achieve success. What if I told you in the midst of it all, everything can fall apart and go towards a direction you had not expected? What if everything fails, a catastrophe arises, a family member goes into a mental crisis, and you end up with a debilitating chronic illness? What if the only thing you could hold onto was your truth during these difficult times? What is your truth? You are probably asking yourself what I mean by that question. What do you hold on to in times when you have no idea what to do about your current situation?

As you read the pages of this book, I would like for you to think about what, or who, has kept you running through the battles of your life. You may encounter different belief systems and different challenges the women collaborating on this book have gone through, but we expose our stories to empower you to not give up when the troubles of life start knocking on your door. In my personal growth, I have learned that our life is a journey in which we must travel with a deep consciousness and understanding of who holds our life up. Have you ever questioned who is the force giving you strength day in and day out? Every time I have fallen, I was reminded of God's promise in Jeremiah 29:11, which reads:

*For I know the plans I have for you declares the Lord, plans to prosper you and not to harm you. Plans to give you hope and a future.*

When I earned my Baccalaureate in Psychology, I incorporated Jeremiah 29:11 in the design on top of my graduation hat. It has been a great reminder of God's promise for my life, even when I didn't have a clue of what career to pursue. Even though I believed with all my heart that God's promise would unveil in due time, waiting was easier said than done. Undoubtedly, in the middle of chaos we tend to see only the negatives in our lives. While I was experiencing debilitating pain, I was also in a state of shock because I considered myself to be very strong and I couldn't understand why this was happening to me. Something kept whispering into my ears and telling me there is a bigger reason for my excruciating, childbirth-like, temporary suffering; it would benefit the wellbeing of many other people suffering from a mysterious chronic illness.

During that time, I endured a few life lessons that I needed to understand before I could move on with my life's purpose. I noticed a pattern of thought in the many books I read; Audrey Hepburn, the famous actress, once said, "We have two hands; one is to help ourselves and the other one is to help our neighbor."

I have always enjoyed serving others without hesitation, but sometimes I came back home empty hearted. I felt like I was expecting to get back the same type of care I was giving to other people. God revealed to me that I was putting my faith in the wrong place and being a blessing to others was enough. This reminded me of my mother's teachings; she continued advising me how Jesus Christ is the only one that could fill any void we may have in our hearts. This made me question my motives. This BIG life lesson has made a huge difference on how I live my life and understanding my purpose.

After reassessing all the resistances in your life, have you asked yourself why you experience these blockages? Are we doing it for our own satisfaction? Are we working towards the improvement of our immediate world? Why are we doing it? Romans 8:28 says, "And we know that all things work together for good to them that love God, to them who are called according to his purpose." I strongly believe God's heart is the most sensitive and tender; anything we do will be noticed. As a follower of Jesus Christ, I proclaim I am not a religious person. For many, this may not be easy to comprehend, but I explain it as having a personal relationship with the creator of the universe and utilizing that relationship to bring blessings to others. This brings joy to God.

You may ask, "How does this tie in with the purpose of this book?" Not all of us figure out our purpose early in life and it is perfectly okay. In any case, many of us, despite our relationship with God, may find ourselves fighting and resisting something in our lives only to find out that the very thing we were resisting may be what our life's purpose is about. It took me a while to figure out what I already knew deep inside was my passion. My passion is teaching and empowering others to be the best they can be. Some way, or another, I repeated these actions. It became very natural for me. I motivated others and made sure those that needed my help received care. It took me a while to understand the many aspects of my passion and how I should proceed. While I went to school to study Psychology I was not sure if I wanted to pursue an actual career in Psychology. Studying four years of psychology helped me out in understanding why people behaved the way they did in the different seasons of their lives. Above all, I do not regret going to school for it, but I surely regret not being more involved with it. This was inevitable because I was continuously sick all the time. Consequently, I was very interested in different wellness programs and decided to take classes in the sciences such as neuroanatomy, medical terminology, and physiology because I knew I ultimately wanted to do something in the wellness arena.

To further explain my passion and purpose, I would like to backtrack to my early years of growing up and mention that as far as I could remember, I was always sick and in pain. I never mentioned this to my friends, nor at school. Everyone around me thought I was perfectly healthy, with the exception of my mother; she took care of me. My body was always expressing pain one way or another. My mother kept telling me she was going to change my name to Dolores! That would be "Ms. Pain" in Spanish because of how much I complained about different parts of my body aching. What's a child to do but cry when in pain? Thankfully, my mother's care has always gotten me back on my feet. I thank my father in heaven for gifting me a mother like her. Never take pain or strange feelings in your body for granted. Always seek professional-functional help with medicine. Sometimes, it is easy to put ourselves on the backburner. By then, it will be too late to prevent chronic conditions that may arise. It happened to me. I waited six months to see a doctor and what a big surprise I got!

Four years after getting married to my best friend, Erick, and learning to adjust to our new life, we decided to move north for a great job opportunity that has opened many doors for us. In 2015, I dealt with the worst pains I could have ever imagined. After so much testing, my primary doctor diagnosed me with rheumatoid arthritis. For those of you who may not know, rheumatoid arthritis is a condition that western medicine has described as an autoimmune disease where the individual's cells attack themselves. When I was hit with the realization of what I had, I experience different emotions. On one end of the spectrum, I finally had a name for my aches and pains, but on the other side, doctors had categorized this as a permanent illness where I would have been required to take pharmaceutical drugs for the rest of my life. This did not sit well with me.

Honestly, I did not know much about this condition until I was diagnosed, and I started to do my research. Those who know me know how much I love digging into science-based research to validate reasoning. Automatically, I asked the rheumatoid specialist about the possible side effects of the medications being prescribed. In turn, the doctor provided me with what I thought was a very long list of side effects, including: gradual bone loss, depression, gradual loss of eyesight, and weight gain, among other things. After carefully analyzing the best course of action on how I wanted to treat my pain and inflammation, I decided I was too young to accept one type of treatment. A feeling deep inside desperately guided me to continue researching my diagnosis and its additional treatments available in the world.

With a thankful heart, I appreciate my primary doctor in Noblesville, IN because she has listened to me and helped me through this process. After months of research and many natural approaches, I finally found doctors in both Manchester, IN and in my home town Miami, FL that treated rheumatoid arthritis, first using a natural approach before relying on pharmaceuticals. I would like to thank both Ralph and Michael Lemus for being the catalyst in jumpstarting my immune system back up. Their motto explains their use of pharmaceutical drugs as an alternative when natural medicine is not working. That is perfectly fine in my book! I believe we should be using a natural route first and if that doesn't work then as a last result its ok to go to the conventional route. Finally, these amazing doctors made sense of what was happening in my body. I am very grateful for them because after receiving great care, I realized my purpose in life, to bring awareness to many suffering with chronic illnesses, such as rheumatoid arthritis and fibromyalgia, and the different approaches available.

After my inflammation and body aches went away so rapidly, I was so shocked that something inside of me kept telling me that I needed to help other people that are suffering how I was suffering before. My growing passion has evolved to help individuals investigate the root of their pains and aches, using actionable steps, such as learning to listen to their bodies.

To make it official, I decided to go back to school to become a nutritional consultant, to start my journey in health care and preventative medicine. This allows me to help so many women who have no idea where their pain is coming from. In addition, I started a community group where everyone supports and motivates each other through the dark shadows of not knowing what to do next. My purpose in this life is supporting and motivating woman as a nutritional consultant and soon to be nutritional therapy practitioner. I help woman make sustainable changes in their lifestyle habits, so they can feel their very best. Everything is personalized and what works for you will be different from what works for someone else. When it comes to your health there is no one size fits all.

To learn more about the specifics of my journey to recovery from chronic illness, head over to www.SMarieFitness.com.

Connect with me and find out the best way we can work together to create a sustainable wellness plan that will jumpstart your road to recovery.

Finally, I want to reiterate that I am not a doctor and to always consult your primary doctor, especially functional doctors, before choosing and proceeding with a treatment. My purpose is to give you the tools to investigate the root cause of your symptoms and help you create a lifestyle where you can feel your very best.

Now it's your turn to tap into your purpose.

*The secret of change is to focus all of your energy not on fighting the old, but on building the new. -Socrates*

Can you identify the resistances in your life? Can you decipher what is holding you back from your purpose? Here is a list of things to incorporate in your life that can help you get a clear perspective of your purpose:

- Pray, fast, and listen for God's purpose for your life.
- Trust that what you want will come in due time but may not necessarily be exactly how you expected it to be.
- Let life guide you and ask lots of questions.
- Do not miss the signs in the circumstances of life.
- Do not resist change. Instead, adjust to what works best for you.
- Identify recurring patterns of mistakes and refuse to give in.
- Embrace life's positive change and be a blessing to others within your capacity.
- Be happy knowing that God's purpose for your life was already established and in due time He will show up.

I pray that you can find comfort in knowing in the middle of it all God has been there and has protected you in the hardest of the situations. There was a time that I had forgotten about God's love for me, but even though I stopped looking for Him, he was still there. If you are not a believer of Jesus Christ, I challenge you to give Him a chance and invite Him into your precious heart. He is there with open arms, ready to lift you up and guide you through the troubles of life. Also know that Life is about continuous change and growing with it. Resisting and overlooking change is resisting your own growth. If you are ready to invite Him for the first, second, or third time, say this small prayer and know that He is ready to work in your life to show you your purpose:

Dear Heavenly Father,

Welcome you into my heart and I confess and repent of my sins to you, oh Lord. I believe Jesus Christ is your son and that he died on the cross at Calvary so that I may be forgiven and have eternal life in the kingdom of heaven. I confess with my mouth that I am born again and cleansed by the blood of Jesus. I give you total control of my life and would love for you to show me your purpose for my life at the time you have chosen. Father, thank you because I am at peace that your will be done in my life in Jesus Name, Amen.

Here's a big hug if you prayed this prayer. If you have any questions or don't know where to turn next, feel free to send me an email at Steph@SMarieFitness.com so that I can send you additional resources that may help you in your journey. Many blessings and remember: When it comes to your health, there is no "one size fits all."

Sincerely,

S. Marie Vargas

# S. Marie Vargas

    S. Marie Vargas is a wellness project manager and nutritional consultant who is dedicated to creating awareness of the health benefits of a preventative medicine lifestyle. She is native of the Dominican Republic, an entrepreneur creative, and supports women and youth empowerment across the different cultures.

    S. Marie received a Baccalaureate of Arts in Psychology from Florida International University with a minor in Communications studies. She is a certified medical interpreter and has worked in numerous medical and educational environments, advocating for patients and students.

    She currently lives in Indiana with her husband, and the joy of their life; their chihuahua, Daisy. She enjoys traveling, visiting the library, biking, and trying new gluten-free restaurants.

# Chapter 4

## THE DAY I MET MYSELF

### By Yashate' Pendergrass

I want to take you on a journey to the time God allowed me to meet myself. For most of my life, the world has judged me. I was known as SHE, teen mom, double divorcee, single mother of two, a failure, broken, and my favorite, "ship wrecked". It wasn't until I truly opened my heart and listened to God's words that I was able to begin my walk into my purpose.

**My background**

My story began the summer of 1977. From the moment the doctor announced, "it's a girl," my siblings began molding who I was. I never seemed to have a clear identity. Being the youngest, everyone simply referred to me as "she", "her", or "the baby". The labels seemed to be sufficient, enough, when people spoke of me. Born to a single mother and a married father, others chose to call me "THAT baby girl".

In 1984, I reached school age. All I wanted to do was fit in with the other girls. Again, I found myself being judged and labeled. My peers described me as the fair skinned, skinny-legged, big headed, dirty brown-haired Girl. While others played in the sand box, I would glaze off into the sky, wondering, "why was I born? Why was I alive?" I never fit into the norm like the other named girls, I was just "her".

In 1994, I earned the title of teen mom. In 1996, my African-American English teacher labeled me as a failure, the teen mother and future drop out. I was the one who couldn't be the homecoming queen because I had a child. I took in every label, insult, and judgment people threw my way and it didn't stop there. In 1999, I was the girl who was the single mother of two sons, that single mother who should be on welfare, that single mother whose sons will be drop-outs and end up in gangs. By 2004 I was the married and divorced single mother of two living in a rural area. By 2013 I had been married and divorced, twice. Oh my goodness, "what a shame". The way people talked about me and referred to me, you would have thought I murdered someone.

After listening to the voice of God, I was led to go off the grid for a while. This was something I did, from time to time, to hear the voice of God without the noise of my friends or family. During this time of solitude I found myself looking back over my life via the eyes of the world. All I could see was the "SHE, HER, TEEN MOM, FAILURE, etc." out of the mouths of the others. BUT GOD... God has me to go back and look at myself through his eyes. Yes, by the end of 2013, I began to look into who "this" girl was; who is this she, her, teen mother, failure, etc. that everyone talks about? I wanted to know her story, her purpose, her assignments in life? Why did God take the time to mold and shape her? Why did God hold back the hands of the enemy and spared her life? Why did God trusted her to bring two amazing sons full of purpose into the Earth? Why did God spend time making this little girl, and better yet, who was this girl? It was at this moment that God began the process of allowing me to meet myself...

## *I Can't Change What They Do;*
## *I Can Change If They Do It to Me*

As a teen mother, I recall feeling like I was always on stage, performing for the world's approval of me. I recall reaching out to my son's father for help with diapers. I was beyond broke and did not have the means to buy anything. To be honest, I couldn't even afford to buy free air. My son's father felt that food for his upcoming birthday party was priority over the need for our son's diapers. The fact that my son's father could not understand the importance of providing for our son was an epiphany from God. I didn't understand God's message at the time because I had yet to meet and understand myself, but I knew in my mind what I had to do. The day of my son's father's birthday party I had a gift for him. I gifted him with the news that we were no longer a couple. He wasn't ready to be a parent at such a young age. I did not have a choice anymore. I couldn't control his lack of parenthood, but I could control him being an unproductive element in my life. Statics suggested I should be a mother on welfare for the rest of my days. These same statistics also suggested my two sons would drop out of school, be in gangs, and/or be inmates for the majority of their lives. At that time in my life, I did not realize how bad the odds were against my family, but I refused to accept the stigma society placed on us without a fight.

Fast forward, to my second marriage. The man I married could have won an acting award for his performance prior to us getting married. A year after our "I do's", however, the show was over and the actor had put down his script. Despite the fact he was a hard worker that provided for his family, financially, he lacked the core ability to love his family with a pure heart. I endured years of verbal and emotional abuse and years of sharing our marriage with some other woman because I was afraid. I spent years of praying, crying, feeling lost, and not knowing who I was. To put it simply, I was a ship wreck. I was afraid of what people would say about me. All the comments and sneers of the past (the she, the single mother of two, the lady that has been married twice) kept hurling in my mind. What would they say? I was lost. I did not see, or understand, how God had his hands on me during this season of my life. Not knowing who you truly are in Christ and your purpose for life, will cause you to put up with chaos and allow yourself to be treated any kind of way. But when you meet yourself, your God-given self, you will change your life, your surroundings and your future.

When you understand who God created you to be, and you begin to grow, you realize you may have to let go of the very people you believed where on your side. I've had friendships that almost took me out with hurt. I recall wondering how a girl or friend could hurt my heart. I did not understand how "so-called friends" would allow me to celebrate their successes, but would not celebrate my successes along with me. It was hard to deal with friends who turned their backs on me, without cause or explanation. I had been willing to lay down my morals and values to fit in with the crown. BUT GOD. I was on my dad's farm one day telling him how I felt. He told me that people will dislike you for no reason. He said, "people will hate you because you're a happy and open-minded person." That was the hardest thing for me to comprehend. I believed, truly, my father had made a mistake in his advice about people. In time, however, I found he was accurate with his guidance.

I could not imagine the calling God had on my life. I could not begin to understand the various seasons of life I had to go through to be molded and shaped for His purpose and His will for my life. Transformation in my life came from not knowing who I was, but seeking who I was created to be. I am grateful to God for presenting me to myself, for the journey is truly empowering. I discovered, I could not control how individuals treated me or how they refuse to celebrate me, but I could control how I permit others to mishandle me.

## When God Spoke

It all begun one warm spring morning as I set on Isle of Palms beach in South Carolina. I noticed the sun was smiling and it seemed the birds where singing a melody just for me. His voice...it wasn't an earsplitting sound or booming vibration...but I knew that it was the voice of God. I knew deep inside my inner soul that my God had begun a new work in me. I have always enjoyed the beach, sitting at the water, listening to the echo of the water break, feeling the wind on my skin, and taking in the energy of the ocean. This day was different. On this day, God began an illustration of my life concerning the beach. In a tranquil fashion, there arose revelation regarding my past, for "God hath chosen the foolish things of the world to confound the wise (1 Corinthians 1:27, KJV)". As I sat on the beach and increasingly opened my heart to the voice of God, I looked and saw people of various colors, shapes, and age standing at the water's edge. I realized that regardless of who stood at the shore, the water never ceases to operate as God had intended it to. Despite the amount of people in the water or what region of the world they were from, the water's responsibility to continuously bring immaculate fresh water to the shores, remained unchanged. At that moment, I realized despite what we see as broken elements of our life, God wants us to recognize that our purpose and assignments remains unchanged. The trials and tests that we endure represents the various people, standing at the waters' edge.

Just like the waters' purpose, our purpose is appointed by God, not man, or what we have endured. It is not validated by who has hurt you, disappointed you, turned their back on you, who walked out on you, or how you think people should treat you. You were born with purpose, just as the sun has a job to warm the earth, to help things grow, and to assist the earth with light for us to see. The sun does not choose which day to shine, nor does it work based on emotions. I realized the sun's purpose is connected to our purpose. God is in control. He made the earth and everything in it, He made you, and He allowed the storms in your life. It is not by chance that we are still alive, still open to our purpose, and still trusting God's plans for our time on earth. He revealed that my walk may be the only example of light for some people. The frequency of my voice may be the "IT" that helps transform a blinded and broken soul into a vibrant, intact individual who is eager to glimpse into their purposeful future.

I realized that not everyone will get healed or delivered within the four walls of a building; therefore, if my kitchen table has to be the alter in which God can transform a life, I say "let God's will be done". If the sun helps to bring light to the world after the darkest of night, so is the same for Kingdom workers. It is our duty to be that tangible person or the prescription in which to treat, heal, and promote growth in hopes of purpose fulfillment. Understand, that our life is not about us or our observation of what should or should not be, it is ONLY about God's purpose for our time on earth. The wind blows upon us all. Some people recognize its cool presence, while others are too busy with their personal agenda. I can relate. I had visited the beach many times before this season in my life, but it was at this appointed time, God chose to converse with my spirit. The wind blew on everyone. The wind did it compete with the sun or ocean, the wind had its own role and purpose. This was a "wow!" moment for me. This revelation highlighted the importance of me knowing who I am and my unique purpose and position in the earth. It is essential for the sun to shine, not to blow. It is also vital for the ocean to come and ebb and flow, not to shine. What I took from this is: we are made to perform as individuals with a particular purpose/blue print designed by God, not to be mixed up with the floor plans of another. The ocean, wind, and sun is available for us all; however, it is dependent upon the person to acknowledge the purpose and utilize each according to their purpose.

I think about seashells, how they occupy the ocean floor. There are millions of shells and each have taken a different path which permits them to wash ashore. Think about it, some shells end up on South Carolina beaches, while others wash ashore on the coast of Florida. How would one explain that each shell has a common home in the ocean but ends up on various beaches around the world? Is it that certain shells where picked up by the oceans current because they were light weight? Maybe some enthusiastic young child picked a shell from the Florida coast and later dropped it during a summer trip to Texas? Who really knows? All I know is, "as God is in control of the seashells' paths, he is in control of ours also." Let Him lead you. How do we justify our common foundation of being born into the earth, being in touch with the same sun, wind, love of Christ, but end up in various locations in life? God has ordered each step. I understand that where I am at this point in my life, is where I am supposed to be. God told me my path was designed for me, stop looking at the blueprints of others. The plan that was made for them was for them, not me. Just as the path of a beautiful breathtaking seashell was strategically planned and timed by God to arrive on the shore of a South Carolina beach, God planning my journey, also.

During my same visit at the beach, I met a new widow. She shared details about her loss, along with her purpose for being at the beach that day. God heard her prayer and knew what she needed on that day to encourage her to press on and trust him. She shared that she was in a bad place after her husbands' death. She was angry, hurt, and did not see purpose for her life. She shared that her husband loved the beach and that he enjoyed the feeling of standing before a new ocean with every tide that came in. God woke something in me with those words. It is true that the waters' edge is composed of fresh new water with every tide. It was an epiphany that the oceans' tides symbolize how God rewards us with morning/a new day in which to let go of the former and embrace the new. The widow came to the beach in search of God. She desired to understand her purpose after surviving the most challenging time in her life. As she shared her story and we walked the beach, she came upon what she said, "was the most beautiful seashell she had ever seen". She knew that this was her answer from God; she understood that her life still had purpose, her answer was in the beauty of a seashell. I heard and saw God in her story. God used her to speak into my life, to bring a deeper understanding of the importance of knowing yourself and your purpose. I do not believe that any old shell would have cast the beauty and captured her heart the way that shell did. I knew that it was vital for me to be in position for the purpose of God, just as the shell was in place for its purpose. God needs each of us to do the same. People are waiting on us. People are hurting, broken, and feeling shipwrecked, but that is not the end of their story. God spoke to me during a day trip to the beach. I now know that wasn't His first time talking to me. I didn't hear God's voice clearly before because I had not taken the time to listen.

## Meeting Myself

A few weeks after my illuminating beach visit, I recall an unexplainable feeling of self- awareness. It was like I had discovered some things about myself that were not new, but seemed like I was discovering them for the very first time. I recall looking in the mirror, as I had done a thousand times before, feeling something was different. I gazed upon a person that looked like me, spoke and sounded like me; however, something had surely changed. Just as God had revealed to me the purpose of the ocean, sun, and wind during my beach visit: it was at this time that God began a work in me. God started the process of introducing me to myself. I had no inkling how my life was about to be transformed. I had lived with myself all my life, but did not truly know who I was. I knew the name that was given to me by my parents, I knew my birth order, and the various labels others placed on me. What I didn't know was who God had created me to be. Before I met myself, I placed restrictions and boundaries on my goals to make others feel comfortable. As God introduced the blueprint for my life and purpose, I began to understand why I carried the title of teen mother, divorcee, single mother, powerless, and incapable. God helped me to realize that everything I needed was already in me, and each title held purpose for the process of me meeting myself.

As I looked in the mirror, God introduced me to the teen mother: I met this sixteen-year old girl who chose to embrace motherhood over running away from her actions and being the judge and jury of life. Society and statistics would have her believe her fate as a young teen mother of two black, male sons in the rural south was destined for failure. However, I witnessed her beating the odds despite what other thought. Despite spoken words, from an unnamed female African-American English teacher, capable of paralyzing this young mother's hope for a recoverable life, she beat the odds. I saw this frail, but strong, sixteen-year-old student refuse to accept the teacher's words of failure and never amounting to anything, instead making her mark in the world. God encouraged me to meet her; she was me, that teen mother who faced the grueling challenges of motherhood, who conformed to the passion of purpose, and not the numerous statistics over her life. "We make statics, statics does not make us"! We hold the passion of purpose, even when were unaware of it. Now that I understand the reason for my journey, I can encourage other teen mothers who may feel that their life is over and they have no purpose on this earth. I can coach her into the elements of self-awareness and how meeting yourself is essential to walking in purpose. It is impossible to walk in the fullness of who you are, when you don't understand the depth of who you are concerning the blueprints of your purpose.

God then introduced me to the divorcee. I was married at a young age, striving to do the right thing as a single mother of two, despite being shipwrecked and disappointed with the outcome of marriage, and being told "no one would want a single mother with two sons". God introduced me to the divorced me, in spite of all the hardships I endured. I was not bitter or angry. I still believed in love because, at this point, I was aware of my worth and purpose. If I never experienced hurt or disappointment, I would have never been able to birth my passion to help and empower others to live and love. I realized that "I can't change what people do, but I can change what they do too me". Once God revealed my purpose, position, worth, and wealth as a woman, I was enthusiastic about sharing my story with others. I know the betrayal of my trust wasn't about me, it was about learning to trust God's assignment for my life. After I met myself, I learned how to be victorious and not the victim.

Over the last few days, God allowed me to meet the single mother: by age twenty-one I had given birth to my second son. I was a "single mother of two". I saw a young mother still excited and hopeful about her future. It was during this season that God was building purpose for my passion. As I looked at the young single mother in myself, I was amazed that she didn't succumb to pity parties. Yes, I had them, but I gave my pity parties a 24-hour time limit. I realized that time was of the essence, people were waiting to hear my story, they needed to attain hope and encouragement for tomorrow. Let me be transparent, before I met myself, before I understood my purpose and assignment in the earth, I was shipwrecked without a GPS signal to find my way back on course. Hello You!!! If you get nothing else from my story, understand that self-awareness is essential for walking out the blueprints for your life. If it was up to the devil, I would have been controlled by the statistics of society. I would have never overcome the title of teem mother to become a registered nurse. I would have never gone from a divorcee to a woman who still believes in love, nor would I have gone from a single mother who could not enlist in the United States military to becoming an officer in the U.S Army Reserve. Now that I have met myself, I understand those seasons of feeling powerless and incapable of being a mother, woman, and wife. I realized I did not need the permission of others to walk in the spirit of love or to be the tangible component of the world's healing process. My potential to change the world was not based upon the previous titles of my life. In fact, each title I held had everything to do with my molding process.

After God's introduction of me to myself, I was different. I was empowered with the blueprint of my life. I understood the reason for the hurt, sadness, disappointments, and shipwreck moments in my life. I had attained a healthier and more enhanced perception of myself. I am no longer subjected to the title of teen mother, divorcee, single mother, or incapable. I have now met YashaTe', the person behind the titles, the lady selected by God to run the race of purpose! The winner of the race is not based upon speed, physical appearance, or ones' ability to endure the heat of the sun. The campaign of the race is chosen by the manner in which individuals perceive the tricks of the enemy. Self-awareness is a pivotal ingredient in establishing and constructing who you are; therefore, seeking the instructions of your maker is vital to meeting yourself and fulfilling your earthly assignment. Our time on earth is limited, we do not have time to spare: someone is waiting on you to walk into the passion of your purpose. I have!!!

## Walking in Purpose

Now that I understand myself, and my passion, I have started to walk in and on purpose. I am now a certified self-awareness life-coach, author, founder of YashaTe Inc., empowerment speaker, community volunteer-organizer, and entrepreneur. I have decided to answer the calling on my life and use the lessons of my life to facilitate others with difficult, but not impossible circumstances. I pray that you would read my story, gain understanding for the dark hours in your life, and decide to live on purpose, because the world needs you. This is just the beginning. Do not quit now!

# Yashate' Pendergrass

    YashaTe' Pendergrass was born in the small town of Kingstree, South Carolina, the youngest of seven children. At the age of sixteen, a senior in high school, Yashate' became pregnant. The last of her friends to explore with sex; she was the first to become a teen mother. Being a teen mother, Yashate' found herself being the topic of hurtful discussions. Her teachers, classmates, so-called friends, and other adults declared failure over her life. For a while, she believed what people said about her. After getting over the hurt, pain, and disapoints of her environment, however, she decided to FIGHT. She decided to fight the negative self-talk within herself. She fought to overcome the degrading, powerless words of others.

Over the years, Yashate' not only had to deal with being a single parent, she also endured a cheating husband, accepting his child as part of their family, a divorce, and a house fire that resulted in her losing everything. Yashate' remarried a man who eventually became, verbally abusive. It was during this time that she realized she was totally unaware of who she was and what her purpose was in life. She felt shipwrecked. That is when God stepped in and saved Yashate' from herself.

God rescued her and her children from a dry season. He saved her from a shipwrecked state of mind. Today, Yashate' is a nurse in the United States' Army Reserve, a business owner, and a public speaker. Yashate' is on a mission to use her voice to help others walk into their fulfillment in life. She is determined to encourage others to reclaim themselves and live again. Through Yashate', Inc. (#MeetUrSelf), she helps individuals move from a state of brokenness, unawareness, and worthlessness to a place of healing, self-awareness, and self-confidence.

My passion is to coach, galvanize, inspire, and empower a tribe of people to be successful, and prolific people of society. Looking back, I would have given a million dollars, to have a program like "Hello YOUniversity" to help me recover from life. I was alone in my pain and disappointments; therefore, my mission today is to be an expert witness to help others through. I currently share a video blog on Facebook each Wednesday entitled Grown Folks, this another way of sharing my story to help others.

I am an overcomer, I am excited to service, and I am BLESSED.

Yashate' Pendergrass

# Chapter 5

## F_CK POSITIVITY: MAKE SHIT HAPPEN!

### By Jessica Mayor

*Positivity is the result of being disciplined, organized, and committed with your mind, goals, and healthy habits - Jess. M.*

So, how does one start writing about one's life? With the hope, that by sharing a simple story, this story will ultimately become an inspirational tool for someone struggling with any life circumstance, be it physical, emotional, or mental?

My life! My life is important, this I know. I wondered, however, if my story was important enough for an audience to find it intriguing? I wanted to share my story for a while now, but thought if I went to an editor and gave her or him my draft, it would never get to a publisher. I am not a famous actress, neither a famous entertainer. I am not a known artist or someone that is widely known in the public eye. Why would anyone want to publish my book?

Whatever you want to call it, light, energy, Jesus, soul or consciousness – I call it God- He tells me that I am of importance and, why not? Why not write about myself? I am part of this world and I can share and provide insightful information about a powerful life – my life. I accept all cultures and backgrounds and, like Dandi Pani says, "Life is a manifestation of where you direct your energy." I want to direct my energy towards a positive life. I am the sum-total of where I have been investing my energy throughout my entire life. I figured out my purpose. I know what and who is important in my life and how to direct this energy towards my goal so that I can manifest it in my life. That means, if I can do it, anyone can.

There is a beautiful message that Maya Angelou spoke in an interview, and is a message I find uplifting for any human who is willing to transform themselves regardless of their ethnicity, social status, mental history and/or physical disability. In a Master Class aired on Oprah Winfrey's network, OWN, Maya Angelou reminded us we are all children of God, and as such, we recognize the same God that made fleas and mountains made us, too. We all share the same qualities and should treat every human being with kindness, as they too, are children of the most high. She reminded us that if some of the greatest people in the world like Mother Teresa or Malcolm X can dare to be bigger than their circumstances, than so can we.

And, so can you! You can try to stretch! Stretch! Stretch yourself! Words that Maya Angelou uses to help us understand how to always go that extra mile. We can all push forward even in hard times, just a bit, so that change can do its magical touch. Transform us! Therefore, here I am, stretching, pushing that limit that I have set in my mind to go past my limitations, because now that I know my disadvantages I can go beyond them. Since one of my flaws is the fear of rejection, what better way to stretch my courage and let go of the stupid fear than by writing this book.

I love reading and writing. Writing is complex and I find it fascinating. I noticed since I was a little girl that I liked words. I wrote short poems about silly stuff like love. I remember being seven, sitting next to my mom at her office and she would hand me pens and papers so that I stay active. She would say –

"Jessica, draw anything beautiful or write something. Always keep busy," so I wrote. I wrote little verses about love that perhaps made no sense, because, really, what can a seven-year old girl know about anything related to love? For some reason, however, I was inclined to write about how I thought love feels.

Words are special. To decide which words are best to use, to place on paper, is sort of a dance...words, comma, and space move together into a sentence that it is calculated to build the finest artwork according to whoever is writing. It becomes a performance. The audience grasps the sense the author is trying to project, then analyzes it according to his/ her own knowledge and personal experience. Thus, words need to be synchronized with one another, seamlessly, to spawn a sentiment that would stir the reader to be hypnotized without missing a beat. It is fascinating! I gravitate to that vibe.

The vibe I am, also, gravitating to is, absolute focus and intention. I have to focus on my goal to continue to improve myself in all aspects of life; financial, professional, spiritual, physical, mental, as well as, intention. When I decided to write this short book, the first question I asked myself was, what is my intention? Is it to get noticed? Is it to talk about myself? What am I really trying to accomplish with this? And my sincere and true answer is, I want to help. I want to be of service, and if by sharing this story someone reaches out to me and I can help, then my intention for this book has been fulfilled. That is beautiful!

## II.

I hope you open your heart when reading this book. Try not to judge the writing or the events written. After all, this is my first book. If there are parts that you do not like or find amusing, know you can just skip them. I just hope you will find encouragement in whatever journey you are going through.

I can tell you I am very fond of pretty things. Since I was little I always liked to watch beauty pageants on the television. My country is obsessed with beauty pageants. Before the United States started with reality drama/beauty shows, my birth country was obsessed with beauty. We have more than 50 beauty contests, if not more. Now that I am older I realized that looking good and your appearance was, and still is, somewhat important to me. I guess you can say I was conditioned to feel and think this way since the majority of what was being displayed on television and in ads was beauty related. To be beautiful, physically, was important and I battle with this, even today. I know it is not the external look that truly matters but from time to time I like to look at myself in the mirror and I do not love what I see. Often, I wish I could modify certain physical traits. The point of this is, I really did not feel I needed to change physically until one day ...someone made a silly remark.

I was born with clubfoot, a congenital condition in which my left foot is twisted out of shape. In other words, the tissues (tendons) connecting the muscles to the bone are shorter than usual. I had a surgery and, from what my mother told me, the doctor advised her to operate on me so I could walk normal. Today, doctors do not need to operate and the treatment is less invasive. Little did my mom know -and I guess back then that was the procedure for my condition – that I was going to have one foot shorter than the other due to the surgery. My left foot is size six and my right foot is size eight. Also, my left calf is massively thin as opposed to my right calf which has more muscle and is stronger. I do not know exactly how but my entire right leg is an inch longer than the left leg, also, which causes my hip and my back to be out of balance. It pains me every time I walk. Because of the right leg being longer than the left, my right side of the body is stronger than my left side. To complicate things, arthritis runs in my family, and I was gifted with this inheritance.

I have Arthritis which is an inflammation of the joints, and when the joints are swollen, they tend to have incomplete range of motion. The range of motion is limited by the swelling within the joint. This is typically associated with weakness in the involved areas. Back when I was little I had to go to physical therapy and, often, had to do exercises only on my left leg. That didn't help much but it created a love for physical activity. I attribute that experience-of going to physical therapy- to my love for all kinds of exercises, whether it be circuit training, high interval training; cycling, crossfit, yoga, pilates, swimming and some sports like tennis. I truly enjoy them all. I feel I always learn a new approach of movement within my own body. But, unfortunately, whenever I want to go beyond any exercise, I am limited. I remember when I was doing crossfit, and I really wanted to compete. I wanted to challenge myself more but my body did not allow me to reach the level I desired because I felt my limitations. But, I feel like I am an athlete. I love physical activities, therefore, I felt a bit upset that I never competed in the Crossfit games; however, I did participate in a Spartan Race. Perhaps my range of motion limits me, and there are certain physical things I struggle doing because they are painful or I am extremely fatigued, but I don't let that stop me. I continue pushing as far as I can go. Even though there are some limitations, I don't let them drift me away from what I enjoy and know is beneficial for my body.

See, the thing is, when you have a physical body like mine, that is not aligned, suffers from arthritis, and the pain is alive all the time, I must exercise no matter what!!!!

LA Fitness, Equinox, Body & Soul, Porky's Gym, Millenium fitness, BluePrint and Coral Gables Crossfit, Calisthenics at Thenx; all those have been studios or gyms that I have used throughout my life. Overall, I think calisthenics, pilates, and yoga are the ultimate physical activity that allows you to be flexible and it gives you access within your body to create massive change. Therefore, you have better quality of life. I suggest anyone who is lacking flexibility or struggling with any physical challenge to try something new once in a while. Witness the changes in the body and mind.

I think fitness has remained constant throughout my life and that consistency is what is most important. Habits are so powerful. Either conscious or subconscious, we do things every day that become habits whether they be good or bad. Many do not realize how powerful habits are. I have learned that by doing something minimal every day, it can change the direction of bad habits. Discipline and consistency are keys! I am more aware of this and try carefully to not start the day with things that do not serve me. Positive habits in the morning are essential to the entire day, as well as, the last hour before going to bed.

At this moment of my life I can truly say I am in a peaceful and humble journey, the most positive and the most honest I have ever been with myself. I am strong, and although I am still trying to figure some things out, I know I am proud of how I have come to understand myself. I write this for two purposes. One, for me to put my life on paper and see how this process of writing evolves. I always dreamed of writing a book and now it is a reality. The second is because I have read many stories and short books about regular people that encountered all sorts of obstacles, and persevered. I found it fascinating how those individuals overcame their own struggles and created a path that was crafted for their own benefit. Their perseverance eventually led to a more positive, healthy, and sustainable life, thus, making their life an example for others to follow. If one person wrote about the difficulty of his/her life, how they conquered their issues and helped someone, then this journey I share, can perhaps bring a sense of hope that someone else can change dramatically, also.

That's what I want. I want my story to be an example to anyone that may identify with my story, feels like they are struggling, and needs hope. Maybe, if at least one person out of 100, feels like my story helps them or moves them and inspires them to take action, then my purpose has been filled. That is enough for me!

### III.

I went through rough and, what some would call, difficult situations in my life. I was sexually molested by a man when I was six years old. Instead of feeling sad I felt shameful; I felt like I had done something wrong. When I was 11 years-old, the boy I liked made fun of me, told me I looked like an alien. He said I was a "weird" girl and he laughed at my leg. I DID have a weird leg and I could not convince myself otherwise. That silly event at a young age made me feel ugly and I thought boys would never like me. I was never aware of my leg being different. No one before this kid, had made me feel different but because I liked him I allowed his opinion to make me feel bad. I felt ashamed, again! I should've punched him in the face or made fun of his ugly breath but I did not. I did nothing because I thought he was right. I had a weird leg. I had to wear skirts because they were the mandatory school uniform. Since that day, I always felt ugly and ashamed for the body I had and I hated skirts. I felt like I was not enough, physically.

Also, since I was little I had severe headaches, suffered from stomach pains, developed gastritis, and eventually, I grew up and many other things unfolded. When I moved to the United States I had to experience things I was not prepared for. I was going to an all girl's Catholic private school in my country but was enrolled in a mixed, public school in Miami when we moved.

I was still playing with dolls at 12 years of age. I lived in a great apartment and had family back in my country, yet in the U.S. I was in a different culture that made me grow up fast. I was not used to seeing young girls at school with boyfriends, wearing miniskirts, and doing drugs. I am not the only person that moved to a different country and had trouble adjusting; I had many classmates that left their countries and went through similar experiences. For me, it was a culture shock. The only family member I had was my mom and my mother would leave me alone in a small efficiency, to fend for myself. I remember the neighborhood was Little Havana- not the best neighborhood to live back then. Mom had to work two or three jobs sometimes, working excessively long hours. I was a loner and lonely. I became a reader, a researcher, and a unique individual. I always felt more mature than other girls. I started evolving into a teenager and started loving listening to music and dancing. I remember watching dance routines for hours and, in my mind, I thought I would become the first Hispanic choreographer. That was my passion but because of my fears, and thoughts of what others would think about me, I did not challenge myself. That is the past, however, and I am not in that place in my life anymore. Soon enough, I became a teenager and I was trying to make sense of my life. I had all kinds of friends in middle school, some were troublemakers, some were real nerds, and some in the middle. I, luckily, did not get into too much trouble at school but I hated middle school. I felt the classes were for third graders. They were extremely easy for me and I never felt like I was learning anything. The classes I had were called E.S.O.L (English for Speakers of Other Languages) classes, which were for kids that did not speak the English language. This class created lazy students. The material was easy and did not challenge me at all, but I did enjoy when lunch came about. Instead of eating I often chose to go to the library and read, read, read. That's how I perfected the language and fell in love with reading and words. Reading was my escape.

Some years passed, I fell in love, and at fifteen I became a mother. After a couple of months of Tony being born, I married my son's father. Tony made me a very happy young mother. He really made me feel like I was never going to be alone in this world. More importantly, he brought a sense of deep purpose into my life. If you dislike the idea of a teenager being a mother, I totally understand. Right now, I am thirty and the thought of my daughter - if I had a daughter – getting pregnant at that age, would freak me out. In all honesty, I cannot lie to you and tell you that getting pregnant as a teenager is right. A teenager does not know how to be a parent. As much as teenagers think they know, they are inexperienced. I have to admit, however, I felt like the perfect mother. I do not know why, but I felt happy. I was not alone; I had an amazing mother that helped me raise my son. Until this day, she is an amazing grandmother. At only 15 years-old I felt sure about having my son. I had made a choice along with my son's father that having the kid was the best choice. I know, intellectually, it makes no sense, but it was a feeling of confidence I never felt before. I knew I wanted to have my baby. Because of Tony I tried to make better choices. When I am no longer alive, I want him to feel like I did the best I could to raise him, the same way I think of my mother. My mother was not perfect but...my God! She is the strongest, the most powerful, and tenacious woman you will ever meet. You cannot bring this woman down. Ever! And that ...is an example of a mother.

I hope one day my son reads this and if he does, this is what I want him to know. Even though I always tell him how much I love him, to describe my sentiment for him in this book makes it a bit more special.

Tony, my sweet son:

I want you to know that you were created with love. Know that you have the capacity to change every aspect of your life that you do not like and wish to improve. Know that there is always space for improvement. Never be complacent, always be inquisitive, and a nonstop adventurer.

Be humble. Always smile even when others are being nasty. This has nothing to do with you; rather with them and their own personal flaws. Make someone's day better by showing them the best of you. Educate yourself about different religions and cultures. Never stop learning. Religions exist for a purpose; each one has rules and traditions that are essential for humans as a way to maintain order and they provide guidelines such as values and ethics. No religion is right or wrong. Religions have truth but is the interpretation of the individual that makes religion flawed. Find your truth. Travel to many countries. Fall in love, get your heart broken. Read, read, read. Interact with people. Be silly. Be playful. Do not say yes to everything and everybody. To know when to say "No" is as powerful as the prayer. Know that in this world we need more humans like these, and you my son, can be an example to the world. I love you, Tony, and whenever you doubt life, pray and thank God. Whenever you accomplish something pray, and thank God, because you are blessed to be alive.

Moving forward to when I was around 18 to 19 years-old, I was feeling tired. Physically, emotionally and mentally, I felt sick. I was always tired without energy. I felt fatigued all the time, even if I had plenty of sleep or not, or if I exercised or not. There was a constant lack of energy that I knew was not normal. I felt unhappy. I was not satisfied with how I felt. I knew money was not the only issue lacking in my life because I always had enough of everything I wanted. This needed attention. I wanted to feel better because I was an adult and needed the energy to work, study, take care of my son, and myself. I was entering adulthood and it was crucial for me to perform 100%, which was not happening. I had finished high school and went to study cosmetology. I found out that doing hair was fun for me. Around 19, I graduated cosmetology and soon enough found work at a beauty salon. I Worked as a bartender as well, for some months, to earn extra money to purchase my first car.

I knew I had to do something. I was not feeling 100%. I never spoke about my sexual assault - only my mother knew – so I felt I needed to talk about it to give it closure. I had personal stuff I needed to share with someone, also. I needed guidance so my general physician suggested I see a professional. He referred me to a psychiatrist. My mom and family did not think going to the psychiatrist was the right path for me to take. I thought they had a point, but praying and going to church was not making me gain energy or feel better. My family from Colombia sent me a book. This book had a natural approach to treat ailments, with certain vegetables, plants, and herbs; which I should have paid more attention to but I was not convinced. I had no discipline on how to treat anything with herbs and did not have the patience to do all that was required. I wanted to feel better instantly and the only suggestion I thought would help at that moment was to go to the psychiatrist. There is a huge stigma about psychiatrists, especially if you come from a Latin family. They said, "doctors do not help and they are only for crazy people". I felt I needed to give it a try and thought, perhaps, a professional would eradicate my fatigue, low energy, and the sadness. I was not crazy. I did not hear voices, nor did I have an issue of cutting, anorexia or bulimia. I never had an alcohol or a drug problem. I just felt I needed professional guidance to understand what was happening to me and why my energy was so low, even though I was eating and exercising.

The doctor suggested talk therapy as well as medication. One pill every day, at a low dosage, that will be increased over time. Seeing him every month, talk- therapy once or twice a week, plus the pill, was becoming expensive. Just the pill for a 30-day supply cost me two-hundred and fifty dollars. The therapy was one hundred and twenty dollars per session and the doctor's visit was eighty dollars. Luckily, I had a stable job and my mother and I lived together. I paid for my medical expenses out of pocket. My health was first and, even though it was pricey, I had to do it.

Becoming an adult was happening; between the ages of 20 and 24 more responsibilities came. Things like learning how to deal with clients, dealing with a divorce, college, co-workers, and conflicts with family happened. It's all part of life. Every person encounters some level of difficulty in all these areas.

Eventually talk-therapy was reduced to once a month and the doctor's visit were every three to six months for the next five years. I cannot lie and say it did not help. Perhaps the fact I looked for an answer and did something about it motivated me and made me feel a bit better, but the tiredness and fatigue continued. I kept telling myself it was not normal that even with the pill I still felt tired and fatigued. I was experiencing things I did not have before, such as; sensitivity to sun, night sweats, rapid palpitations, lethargy, blurred and changes in vision, dizziness, faintness, emotional numbing, chest pains, extreme sweating on hands and armpits, lack of focusing, and forgetting what I did in the morning. I could not even recall what I had eaten in a day. I felt like a zombie; meaning, I could just sit in a chair for hours and experienced nothing. No thinking, no feeling, as if I was dead, is kind of hard to explain but these new things I was experiencing, I knew, was not me. I did not have any of these issues before taking the pill. I explained this to the doctor but the answer was always the same! "That," he said, "was the side effect of the pill and, also part of my ailment". He said, I would be taking the pill forever. The doctor explained to me that the same way a diabetic has to take medicine to control the diabetes forever, I too, would have to take this pill to control sadness for the rest of my life. I explained to him I still felt fatigued and tired and that the pill was supposed to help me with this, which is why I agreed to take the pill in the first place. He insisted a higher dose was needed and that I needed to accept that I would be feeling like that forever.

Well ...guess what? That was not going to happened with me! I think I have a rebellious streak and when he said, "Jessica, you are going to take this pill forever", I said to myself, "never!" I was angry. I wanted to punch something. I remember the last visit to this doctor. I told him that my biggest concern at that moment, was my concentration. I was having trouble focusing when reading and when engaging in a conversation with my friends, clients, or co-workers. It was hard for me to focus on any subject. My situation was out of control and that is why I had to mention this to the doctor. He suggested two pills, one for my concentration and one for anxiety. Anxiety is a normal feeling. I don't think an "anxiety pill" helps at all but that was his suggestion. He also said if I couldn't sleep he could give me a prescription for that, also. According to him, I could sleep without a problem because the side effects of combining all three pills that he was saying I should take, might prevent me from sleeping. I could not believe what he was saying to me. There was no point of talking anymore. I left and I ripped the prescriptions apart. I decided not to continue taking the pill. I had tried to stop taking the medication before, twice actually, by taking it every two to three days apart. When that last visit happened, I discontinued taking the medication altogether.

I also want to add that there was a moment where he changed me to a different pill, to a less expensive one; the generic form. I took the generic medication for three days and it was a terrible sensation. I experienced itchiness on my skin, my mouth was dry all the time as if I didn't consume any water and, the worst of it all, it made me feel suicidal. I remember coming from work feeling nauseous, a heaviness in my body that's hard to translate it into words, as if I had worked for 24 hours straight without sleeping. I went to the room and started writing a letter to my son, saying good bye to him. I wrote him, and told him to never feel guilty because I had taken my life.

After I read it, I noticed how stupid and absurd I was. How in the world could I make my son go through something like that? I threw away the letter and the next day I went to the doctor's office. He changed the pill to the one I had before. I also did research online about this specific medication and many individuals were sharing the same side effects and struggles that I had experienced. On the third time I stopped the medication cold turkey. I do not recommend the cold turkey approach but I was tired of taking the medication and feeling worse than when I had started.

By the age of 26, I think it was 2013, I knew I was going to face a lot of difficulty by stopping the medication. I had personal stuff going on that exacerbated my life. I had read a lot of clinical studies and read people's stories that showed they struggled a lot. That was going to happened to me and I was willing to go through it. I wanted to quit that medication. I saw enough evidence of the long-term effects of the medication and I did not want to put that toxic in my body anymore.

I feel if I write about my most personal part of my life, someone can identify and have a bit of faith and optimism that, hereafter, it gets better. With discipline, organization, commitment, being absolutely honest with yourself, with no mediocrity and zero tolerance for negativity, habits shift and life can be reinvented. Life is many things except a straight line. To learn how to live with joy is the responsibility of the individual. No one is perfect and each person in this world deals with situations differently. Some are born without health issues and others have predisposed conditions or backgrounds that limits certain things in their lives. I 've learned that I am responsible for me, and I must learn to make adjustments in my life. Why? and How? are important questions to ask oneself and when the answers arrive, they will lead to improvement in all aspects of life; mental, physical, financial, and spiritual.

By the time I was 27, I had quit the job I had for over 10 years. Not being disciplined, organized, and committed to my personal life, plus the side effects of the pill and quitting cold turkey, my life spiraled. It was after this – following situation you will be reading – that the process of self-care and self-acceptance began. I eventually sought out my journey so that I could heal, flourish, and grow.

That year was rough. I admitted myself to a suicide clinic. I spent three days in that place. I was surrounded by people that had troubled minds. Some spoke to themselves, others cried a lot, and others laughed, hysterically. When the time came to go outside the room I tried to stay in but I was forced to be with everyone and go to the patio to get air. Here, one woman and a man, in particular, caught my attention. There - at the patio- I was sitting on a bench and was approached by the woman and other individuals. She was an old lady, around 50 or 60 years old. She was a funny and friendly lady. She would tell stories about her life, her beautiful kids, and she even gave me great advice as if she was a therapist. The man that caught my attention was in this group. He spoke like a regular person, was around 40 years old, and was physically fit. Energetic and friendly he, too, was sharing his story. He said he never slept more than five hours. He was prescribed four or five medications. One for his depression, another one for anxiety, another one to make him go to sleep and I cannot remember what the other ones were for. Every day for the past year, he had to take four or five pills to balance his brain.

That was his doctor's orders, but he kept saying he felt worse than before taking the pills. He was not good at all. Some of the people there were heavily medicated, had gone through a lot of trauma, and others had real mental challenges. I felt so out of place. I admitted myself to this clinic because at home I was not able to get out of the negative thinking and I had hit rock bottom. I did not want to live anymore but I was not going to harm myself. I had to admit to myself that I needed to do something! One thing I found out inside this place is that I would never take medication again. I saw first-hand what the pills can do to a person. There I realized and I was convinced even more of the horror stories I had been reading; that the damage medications can cause is dangerous. It is damaging because the medications can create new, additional health issues. I knew I was never, ever going back to a place like that. I left the clinic. I went home and many significant things happened. I knew I was not going to do anything against my life. I still had faith, a small fraction to say the least, but I had it. My son is one of the reasons I had to have hope. I cannot fathom the thought of my child not having his mother and the guilt and the absence he would feel if I committed suicide. Maybe, I have a calling, I don't know. I do believe, however, the difficulty I encountered was to show others that it is possible to make it, even if you are diagnosed with certain challenges. When I left the clinic, I had no job and I felt pure shame. Everyone I knew was doing well in life and there I was feeling like a disappointment, a failure, a weak link in society. I had put my wonderful mother, my son and myself, in a terrible financial situation. My mom was a trooper and she did the best she could to uplift my spirit. She was very tough with me. She is the only one that knew what I was going through. Not even my closest friends knew I had admitted myself to a clinic. What a loser! I thought. Why would any person be friends with me after finding out I had such a weak mentality? But God showed me the purpose of my struggle. I had to go through all of it, and I participated in this tough battle, so that I could have a better relationship with Him- God-, with my mother, and with myself. Luckily, I had real friends, not many, but three, in particular, helped me feel better. My best friend, saw me and saw my struggle, mentally and financially, and helped me with money and other events that led me to see the light. God, my mother, my son, my best friend, friends, my will to transform my life, and recognizing my flaws made me change drastically.

I want this, to be understood. The reason I am putting my story on paper is not because I liked what I was going through, because I was proud of what I went through, nor because I enjoyed going through it. I am doing it because I want to be honest to myself and others. Because the real purpose of this book is to make an impact in someone else's life. If I can feel, live, think, and remodel my being after difficult hardships, anyone can! I do not seek attention. I do not need anyone to feel sorry for me. Feeling sorry for others or for one self is a handicapped feeling that debilitates the mind and soul. Instead, pray. Pray for the individual and send them positive energy. If you don't pray, at least think of them and send them your good wishes with your thoughts. It does something!

### IV.

No one wants to die. Everyone wishes to live. Some people end up killing themselves. Some people have family, education and money, yet they are dead. Some do not have these things, yet they are dead. It is a complex subject. Robin Williams and the singer from Linkin Park are examples of people having mental challenges that resorted to suicide. I could talk about them and the reasons why I think this keeps happening, but that will be in another book.

To conclude this chapter, I will add that mental health is a complex field to talk about. I speak from my experience. From different articles and books that I have read, as well as clinical studies and social media groups I found on the internet, I know there are many alternatives to treat many illnesses rather than just taking a toxic pill full of contaminants. I, honestly, cannot fully blame the doctor for prescribing me a pill and offering more medication (a solution which he thought it could benefit me). After all, it is a society that is driven by capitalism, consumerism, and fast target solutions. Therefore, doctors are taught to quickly fix patients, and patients, consumers, expect a fast solution. An alternative, the opposite, is to look for the root cause of the issue and eliminate it in a pace that is steady and long-lasting.

Looking for the root cause of the issue takes time and unfortunately, money. Here in the United States, if you want a regular doctor, a holistic/functional/natural doctor, or any of these, they will all cost you about the same amount of money. Medical tests, doctor visits, vitamins, supplements, prescriptions, are all pricey and hurts people's pockets. This healthcare system will take time to change. Thus, what I can do in the meantime, is to inform others of their options. I value prevention. It is helpful to eat nutritious food, create healthy habits, become fully committed to your well-being, cut all negative media outlets and people out of your life. It must be done, drastically, your health must be a priority. You must put yourself first when it comes to becoming better and feeling great. Every single day it must be done, no resting. Taking steps, every day, is the only way to shift, to dramatically change your mentality, your behavior, and the feelings will follow. It is not easy, I went through it. If you or someone you know is not at their best, know that I am here. I am, in a way, a survivor. I am here cheering, praying, and willing to act with you, or whoever, is going through a difficulty. We are not alone. There are a lot of natural approaches which, ultimately, are the most effective. They take time but they are a more, sustainable, balanced way of life. Prevention is happening. People like me, and millions of others, are sharing their story so others can find other alternatives to feel better and get healed. There are many other reasons why a person may be feeling sad, or why a person cannot function at their best. It could be caused by a multitude of things, for example: hormonal issue; thyroid not working properly, adrenal fatigue, a gut problem, anemia, lack of vitamin b12 or other vitamins, or a mineral depleted in the body. It could be an autoimmune disease like arthritis. It is known that regular use of painkillers, regular use of antibiotics, infections, inflammatory bowel disease, Gluten hypersensitivity, all affect the body in many ways.

## V.

My second book that goes into detail about mental health is in the works. Meanwhile, this book has done its job. Strictly speaking, it is up to the individual to find out what is the best for him or her. To improve and maintain that great feeling utilize and embrace all the tools gathered so the mind, the body, and the soul work in synergy, therefore, shaping the ultimate balance that the one seeks. I must say, when I started writing I did not even know I was going to actually write the book and have it published. I started writing with the hope that one day I would be able to share my story and develop my writing skills. It is going to sound cliché but I asked the universe and the universe replied with a resounding "yes!" Thank you for reading and taking the time to finish it all. It took many weeks and I am happy with the result. May you continue to grow, find your truth, and live at your maximum potential. Be Well!

Om Shanti! Namaste.
Jess M.

You have to walk the steps yourself from darkness to light. Everyone is seeking happiness. When you water the root of a tree, that water naturally extends to every leaf, and every branch and every flower on the tree. So, when we actually find the origin of our true pleasure, and when feeling the infinite, sweet love that God has for us and in realizing our potential to love God...that love, naturally extends to all living beings

Excerpts from: The Srimad Bhagavatam -The essence of the Vedic literatures.
*Netflix * - On Yoga: The Architecture of Peace

# Jessica Mayor

Jessica Mayor comes from a country that is celebrated for gold, emeralds, coffee , flowers, and beautiful people. She is from the city of Bogota, Colombia. At the age of twelve she traveled to the United States with her mother and has lived in the sunshine state for the past 20 years. She currently lives, and enjoys living, in Palm Beach County. She is a professional hairstylist. She is also a mother, a wife, a friend, a yogi, an author, a fitness lover, a "wannabe" chef with a creative, curious, and adventurous spirit.

If you, or anyone you know, is struggling with any mental health issues, know that you are not alone. There are treatments and approaches that can be tailored to the individual; from holistic, to functional, to integrative. Mental health is just as important as physical health. Let us be a bit more understanding of each other and if you have never experienced any struggle with mental health, you can still practice empathy and compassion for others.

The pathos of life is, as we all know, life cannot always be perfect. There will be challenges. Americans are obsessed with positivity. This is not a bad thing, but perhaps a more realistic approach is to consider what the tittle invites one to do. "F_ck positivity" simply means : Get up! You will fall because life is not perfect. So, do whatever it is in your power to move past the pain. Self-care and self-acceptance must be a priority and ...write the next chapter of your life.


Connect with me :
   @f_ckpositivity
Mayor.ja@yahoo.com

| | |
|---|---|
| Filename: | Passion to Purpose Final (Chrita) |
| Directory: | C:\Users\Chrita Paulin\Documents |
| Template: | C:\Users\Chrita Paulin\AppData\Roaming\Microsoft\Templates\Normal.dotm |
| Title: | Passion to Purpose Collaborative |
| Subject: | |
| Author: | Chrita Paulin |
| Keywords: | |
| Comments: | |
| Creation Date: | 7/30/2018 2:05:00 AM |
| Change Number: | 42 |
| Last Saved On: | 8/22/2018 9:14:00 AM |
| Last Saved By: | Chrita Paulin |
| Total Editing Time: | 653 Minutes |
| Last Printed On: | 8/22/2018 9:15:00 AM |

As of Last Complete Printing
    Number of Pages: 87
    Number of Words: 21,657 (approx.)
    Number of Characters: 123,447 (approx.)

www.ingramcontent.com/pod-product-compliance
Lightning Source LLC
Chambersburg PA
CBHW060849050426
42453CB00008B/914